Table of Contents	Inhaltsverzeichnis	Sommaire

General information about WASARASA with particular emphasis on colour SARASA prints on paper

by Kamon Yoshimoto

For some time now, many people outside Japan have been aware of the existence of SARASA textiles, as they are known. The patterned cloth, a Japanese product, is also often called WASARASA. (In the Japanese language, the prefix "wa" is employed to denote "Japan", "Japanese", etc.)

Legend relates that "WATARI NO SARASA" textiles, from which the SARASA patterned-cloth tradition later developed, were first brought to Japan by Dutch, Portuguese and Chinese traders in the time between the end of the Muromachi period up to the twilight of the Momoyama period and the beginning of the Edo era. (Another theory, however, holds that the origins of SARASA date back to the Asuka or Nara periods).

Whatever the case may be with regard to when the SARASA tradition really began, it is certain that the import of these textiles, through the free port of Hirado in Nagasaki and the trading island of Deshima, reached a high point starting with the Momoyama period and lasting until the beginning of the Edo era. This applies both to the quantity of material imported as well as to the variety of different designs employed.

The proof is to be found in the various trading records of the time, which never fail to mention SARASA textiles as one of the main imports, along with velvet, calico, edging, and similar materials.

An examination of these documents on the "import of printed weaves" yields a number of rather different written denotations for the phrase "SARASA cloth". Although all are pronounced in the same way, there are several ways of writing it, for example with two or sometimes three Chinese pictographs.

Methods of recording the concept "SARASA" in Katakana characters also differ. (Katakana is the indigenous Japanese alphabet). Many interpretations and theories have been formulated to explain the existence of such a broad variety of written denotations, but there is no truly precise explanation.

The hypotheses that have been forwarded to date include the following:

1. The word SARASA derives from the name of a place in India.
2. The word originates from the Dutch.
3. The root of the name is originally Portuguese.
4. SARASA is a term from a southern Japanese dialect.
5. The patterned textiles must have originated in the Saracen empire.

Many such theories have circulated among philosophers and scholars for some time now, but none of them can be described as conclusive. The only generally accepted theory is that there is no generally applicable theory, and one soon tends to speak of the mysterious nature of the textiles.

A few people have lately expressed the opinion that SARASA might be an international industrial term for a pattern, whether of purely Japanese or foreign origin. A question posed to foreign visitors or guests about the Japanese word "SARASA", however, or even about the anglicised description, "Sarasatic Pattern", will generally elicit blank stares, except among foreigners who have been residing in Japan for some years. This is because the textiles which Japanese know as SARASA cloth are called by many different names in other countries, for example printed textiles, printed cotton textiles, patterned cotton weaves, or calico painting. In Indonesia the term is "Batik", while the English speak of "chintz".

But to return to the origins of the SARASA tradition, there is no doubt whatsoever that the radically new and splendid patterns of WATARI NO SARASA textiles imported from Europe and China inspired changes in many areas, as did the curiosity of their wild and unconstrained coloration. The reverberations could be seen in the forms and arrangements of ornaments, designs, and clothing patterns, which had until then been exclusively stamped by the Japanese sensibility. But the effects also extended to pictorial depictions of flowers and birds, and even impacted upon traditional, strictly realistic textile technology, which was designed to reflect the harmony of nature and landscapes. Indeed, the very thinking process of the Japanese, which is very difficult to lay down, underwent an awakening. It is certainly no understatement to observe that these imports blew a fresh wind into the world of Japanese patterned weaves. As is well known, their subtle influence worked upon later muslin patterns and the padded Japanese garments known as KOSODE.

Seemingly all at once, SARASA textiles became a coveted and admired implement of fashion. Priced far too exorbitantly for the general population, they were mainly reserved for princes (daimyo), nobles, higher-ranked knights, and wealthy merchants. Beyond this they were employed ornamentally for the luxurious clothing associated with the art of the tea ceremony. Many a worthy samurai or renowned Master of the tea ceremony possessed the fine weaves. But the prohibitive prices kept them as out of the reach of common folk as a flower at the peak of a high mountain.

The various types of imported SARASA textiles (WATARI NO SARASA) of this period came from countries as diverse as India, Siam, Persia, Holland, Java and China. Each kind was named for its land of origin. They were furthermore sorted into many categories according to their nature and the mode of production employed. Of those pieces which were hand-drawn or made using wood-block techniques, the greater number tended to come from India, Persia, and China. The SARASA material imported from Indonesia was mainly dyed by the Batik process, while the colours of the Dutch and Portuguese textiles were usually impressed through the use of copper plates.

The SARASA goods which were most popular among connoisseurs and collectors were primarily decorated with leaf, grass, or animal patterns — birds, fish, insects and the like. But a warm reception was also reserved for motifs incorporating dolls, subtle patterns, tendrils, hieroglyphics, or depictions of religious scenes and legends. Each of these ornamental arrays conveyed something of the native landscapes or the national character of the country of origin.

Whenever a foreign merchant trader carrying diverse commodities from Europe, China, or other countries alighted in port, a market would be opened up for the shipment. Entrance was restricted to those who had acquired a special permit beforehand. Clients could arrange appointed times to inspect the goods, and there was a continuous coming and going of busy Europeans and Chinese, while Japanese civil servants, translators and licensed sales personnel diligently carried out their duties.

Once a bazaar with a strong foreign flair was initiated on the island of Deshima, the lively hustle and bustle could be experienced outside the appointed times as well.

Originally, the patterned SARASA weaves were cotton prints, but there were also brocades, Chinese woven goods, and magnificent, luxurious silks of extraordinary weave. On special request the material could be decorated with embroidery or gold leaf. Patterns from imported SARASA goods (WATARI NO SARASA) might also be employed on domestically produced orders.

The tradition of JIMBAORI, a kind of armoured lining worn as a cover over a warrior's breastplate, was especially valued by princes and commanders, and has survived to this day. With the intention of cowing opponents during a confrontation without needing to utter a word, splendid and curious patterns were designed for each warrior. The expectation was that enemies would collapse the moment they glanced at the depictions of large felines with powerful bodies. When the warriors went into battle, the patterns and colours of the armour were expected to convey a correspondingly greater threat. Next to the traditional names on the armour, there were pictures of Chinese lions, dragons, tigers, or monsters, each obviously intended to be a demonstration of naked power.

In the changing course of history there came calm and peaceful times as well, and such powerful and weird things disappeared, as did the terrible demon masks. But the simple people of the cities, who lived in a completely different milieu than the nobility and wealthier classes, and who retained a deeply-rooted sensibility for keeping tradition and sticking to their own understanding of beauty, continued to view the over-lively and exotic SARASA patterns from a distance. They restricted themselves to merely admiring the SARASA textiles they saw employed as high fashion on the street and in ceremonial costume, and maintained their doubts about wearing such things themselves. If some circumstance led to their possessing a clearly rare work of SARASA textile art, they tended to only wear it under a kimono, or made hidden cuff pockets out of it. SARASA textiles of pure silk might end up being used as stuffing for a HAORI, a kind of Japanese coat designed to be worn over a kimono in the cold seasons.

But by the final stage of the Tokugawa period (1853 – 1867) simple folk had also come to appreciate SARASA patterns. Financially powerful textile dealers, curious wholesalers searching for greater profits, and the up-and-coming tailors of Western clothes co-operated in the creation of a new, indigenously Japanese SARASA form, known as WASARASA. This late development fused the exoticism of imported SARASA textiles with the well-known patterns of traditional Japanese YUZENZOME (a time-honoured dyeing technique in which glue was used to cover the individual materials).

For this reason the forms we here describe as "WASARASA" were also called "YUZEN SARASA" or "SARASA YUZEN". Clearly the main intention underlying the creation of this new textile category was to market material that the broadest segment of the population could afford.

It was an age of reform, echoing changes in cultural forms abroad. The marvellous and inexpensively produced WASARASA thus appeared at a time when people everywhere were searching for new sensations. The new fashion wave emanated from Edo throughout the other cities and all the way into the country, and was soon established.

Beyond this, a group of designers who were living in Kyoto at the end of the Edo period developed and manufactured their own form of WASARASA. But in this case, it is generally held that the splendid materials they created exceeded even the traditional imported SARASA goods in significance. The Kyoto designers were centred around the Horikawa district and were experts in the old stencil coloration techniques known as KATAZOME. Over time they copied nearly all the known patterns of imported SARASA textiles – a monumental work. There were several thousand kinds of such patterns.

A few designers adopted the practice of making paper prints of the patterns that could then be easily filed away for later reference. Unfortunately very few of these sample pattern collections have survived to the present, but using those that remain for new creations is being considered in some quarters.

Once the troubling time that brought about the end of the Edo period and triggered the Meiji restoration was over, Western culture literally flooded into the country and resulted in sudden, often radical reforms in the habits of everyday life among the common people.

At the conclusion of the Meiji restoration of 1868, a great cry for cultural renewal arose from all sides and within all sectors of society. This naturally had significant effects on the style and general understanding of clothing. Both men and women soon took great pains to adopt fashionable lifestyles and became interested in Western dress. A special flair was particularly associated with Western girls' fashion, and product names like "Wardrobe for Elegant Ladies" seduced people into desiring such innovations.

The arrival of Western fashion coincided conspicuously with noticeable advancements in the manufacture of WASARASA textiles of purest silk. These, together with especially fine SARASA cotton prints, were in great demand for use as material in the making of Western clothing. They appealed to the style of the upper classes, but also found an echo among the common folk, and provided colour and accent to accompany the cultural renewal of the people and the nation. Starting with underwear for ladies and gentlemen, the material was soon being crafted into everyday objects such as parasols, scarves, carrying cases, purses, and the like.

The liveliness that was to be observed at the constant balls and banquets of the Meiji period, where young women of the upper classes could be seen dressed in evening gowns of SARASA material with flowery ornamentation and offering their hands to Europeans for a dance, would have been simply inconceivable just a few years before the collapse of the BAKUFU (pre-Meiji) system. It is no exaggeration to describe such a scene as emblematic of an entirely new system of values.

It is interesting to consider how it was through the free-trade ports of Deshima and Nagasaki that the adoption of occidental culture, art and science was made possible. Observing the then-modern phenomenon of SARASA textiles with imported patterns, we today still feel a secret connection. This is a natural reaction to the mysterious fact that the SARASA fashion was a catalyst in bringing about the second removal of the curtain hiding Japan from the world, and this after 400 years of isolation.

From the beginning until the middle of the Meiji period, provincial cloth dealers, retailers and import/exporters distributed advertising leaflets extolling the virtues of Western SARASA textiles, occidental calico, and imported clothing in general. They created kimonos, linings and HAORI stuffing out of purest silk SARASA. Cotton YUZEN SARASA were formed into carrier bags and futon upholstery, and incorporated into the OBI belts used with traditional Japanese clothing. Regardless of which province or provincial district, much the same products were being sold.

In Kyoto, as we saw above, starting at the end of the Edo period and continuing well into Meiji times, work on the development of WASARASA proceeded with vigour. Meanwhile, in Edo, which is today called Tokyo, the so-called EDO SARASA was also coming into being. This handcrafted art was carried out by masters of EDO SARASA, who were in possession of especially refined techniques of stencil dyeing. Some of their descendants maintain the inheritance and traditions of the old SARASA masters, and are luckily still enjoying the best of health.

In my opinion, one should never forget that it is through the peculiar technology of SARASA, and despite the strenuous course of study necessary to practise it, that a great many artisans still support themselves. Through all the social changes that have occurred, they continue to carry out their art in relative poverty and in keeping with the traditions of country life. I wish to mention only a few of their renowned products, each named after the area in which they are produced: Kagoshima Sarasa, Nagasaki Sarasa, Sendai Sarasa, Akita Sarasa, Edo Sarasa, and Hirokawa (or Kyoto) Sarasa.

The stencil-dyed SARASA paper collections (Katazome sarasamoyo kami) also covered in this book were largely preserved by an artisan whose family has lived in the Hirogawa district of Kyoto since the end of the Edo period. Some of his pieces are today in the safekeeping of the Society for the Historical Research of Textiles. To supplement our documentary account of the many transformations in the history of SARASA textile patterns, some of these papers were picked out and photographed for this book. This was above all done in order to provide artisans with an information resource to assist in their continuing work.

The stencil-dyed pattern papers were produced according to a special process by exceptionally skilled masters of the art. Several paper stencils would be placed one on top of the other, in order to create a particular print pattern. Sometimes up to 20 or 30 stencils were required for a single pattern. All of the samples of dyed pages pictured in this book originated in the period from the end of the Edo era until the middle of Meiji times. Their creation was a preliminary step preceding the pressing of the textiles themselves.

The paper pattern pages served as test prints. They were also used as references for creating other patterns and as samples in store displays. However, they were almost never offered for sale as decorative paper, unlike CHIYOGAMI art, for example.

This book is intended as an overview of the historical WATARI SARASA and WASARASA patterned textile inheritance in a clear and concrete fashion. The different forms and classical motifs are depicted in 759 colour pictures. Nonetheless, this book is being published not for use in theoretical studies, but much more in the hope that it will serve as a small impetus for all those who might use their improved understanding of the long-forgotten works and achievements of the old masters in order to create things new and beautiful.

Allgemeines über WASARASA – mit dem Schwerpunkt auf farbig gedrucktem SARASA-Papier

von Kamon Yoshimoto

Viele Menschen, die nicht in Japan leben, wissen bereits etwas von der Existenz sogenannter SARASA-Stoffe. Bei diesen gemusterten Stoffen handelt es sich um ein japanisches Produkt, welches auch oft als WASARASA bezeichnet wird. (Diese Namensgebung erklärt sich aus der Verwendung der japanischen Vorsilbe „wa" für die Bedeutung „Japan, japanisch etc.")

Ursprünglich, so heißt es, sei das „WATARI NO SARASA", aus welchem sich später das besagte SARASA entwickelte, vom Ende der Muromachi-Zeit bis zur Momoyama- bzw. Anfang der Edo-Zeit über die Handelshäfen der Holländer, Portugiesen oder Chinesen nach Japan gebracht worden. Es gibt auch eine Theorie, der zufolge SARASA auf die Asuka- oder Nara-Zeit zurückzuführen sei.

Fest steht, daß der Import von SARASA über den freien Hafen von Hirado nach Nagasaki/Deshima seit der Momoyama- bis Anfang der Edo-Zeit seine Blütezeit erlebte, sowohl in quantitativer Sicht als auch im Hinblick auf die Vielzahl der verschiedenen Design-Variationen.

Diese Tatsache geht aus den verschiedenen Handelsaufzeichnungen der damaligen Zeit hervor, in denen SARASA-Stoffe neben Samt, Kaliko, Borten und ähnlichem stets als eine der Importwaren erwähnt werden.

Allerdings findet man in diesen Dokumenten über die „Einfuhr von bedruckten Webwaren" recht unterschiedliche Schreibweisen für den Begriff des SARASA. So existieren bei jeweils gleicher Aussprache mehrere Schreibweisen mit zwei oder drei chinesischen Schriftzeichen sowie diverse Wiedergabemöglichkeiten in Katakana, den rein japanischen Schriftzeichen.

Bezüglich des Ursprungs dieser SARASA-SARASA-Muster der Europäer und Chinesen sowie der unterschiedlichen Schreibweisen des Wortes SARASA existieren verschiedene Interpretationen und Theorien, aber eine wirklich präzise Erklärung gibt es nicht. Einige dieser Erklärungsversuche seien hier genannt:

1. Der Name SARASA entstamme einer indischen Ortsbezeichnung.
2. Das Wort habe seinen Ursprung im Holländischen.
3. Die Bezeichnung stamme ursprünglich aus Portugal.
4. SARASA sei ein Wort aus einem südlichen Dialekt Japans.
5. Es handele sich um gemusterte Stoffe aus dem Sarazenenreich.

Viele dieser Theorien zirkulierten unter Philosophen und Gelehrten, aber keine davon ist als endgültig zu bezeichnen. Die einzige allgemein anerkannte Theorie ist, daß es keine allgemeingültige Theorie gibt, und man geneigt ist, von einem Mysterium der Stoffe zu sprechen.

Neuerdings gibt es auch Leute, die die Meinung vertreten, SARASA sei ein internationaler Fachbegriff für ein Muster und stamme entweder aus dem Ausland oder sei ein rein japanisches Wort. Befragt man allerdings ausländische Gäste oder Besucher, die sich für kurze Zeit in Japan aufhalten, nach dem japanischen Begriff SARASA oder der englischen Bezeichnung Sarasatic Pattern, so erhält man in der Regel – mit Ausnahme von Ausländern mit langjähriger Japan-Erfahrung – keine Antwort.

Dies ist darauf zurückzuführen, daß das, was die Japaner als SARASA bezeichnen, im Ausland die unterschiedlichsten Namen trägt. So etwa Printed Textiles, Printed Cotton Textiles, Patterned Cotton Weaves oder Calico Painting. In Indonesien spricht man von Batik, und den Engländern ist Chintz ein Begriff.

Ohne jeden Zweifel bewirkten die völlig neuen, prachtvollen, importierten SARASA-Muster der Europäer und Chinesen sowie die Kuriosität der wilden und ungezwungenen Färbung dieser Muster Veränderungen in vielen Bereichen. So z.B. in der Gestaltung der bislang von japanischen Empfindungen geprägten Ornamente, Designs und Bekleidungsmuster sowie in den bildhaften Darstellungen von Blumen und Vögeln oder in der überlieferten realistischen Technik, mit welcher die Harmonie von Natur und Landschaft wiedergegeben wurde. Auch kam es zu einem Erwachen in der nur schwer abzulegenden japanischen Denkweise. In gewissem Sinne kann man sicher sagen, daß diese Importe frischen Wind in die japanische Welt der bunten Webmuster gebracht haben. Denn es ist bekannt, daß sie auch einen sanften Einfluß auf die späteren Muster des Musselins und der wattierten japanischen Gewänder (KOSODE) ausübten.

Mit einem Mal wurden SARASA-Stoffe zu einer begehrten und bewunderten Modeerscheinung. Unerschwinglich für die normale Stadtbevölkerung, waren sie jedoch hauptsächlich Fürsten (Daimyo), Edelleuten, hohen Rittern und wohlhabenden Kaufleuten vorbehalten. Des weiteren wurden sie als Zierde oder luxeriöse Bekleidung für die Kunst der Teezeremonie benutzt und befanden sich im Besitz von namhaften Samurai-Familien und Zeremonienmeistern der Teekunst. Aufgrund ihres hohen Preises blieben sie jedoch für das einfache Volk ebenso unerreichbar wie eine Blume auf dem höchsten Berggipfel.

Die verschiedenen importierten SARASA-Sorten (WATARI-SARASA) der dcmaligen Zeit kamen aus Ländern wie Indien, Siam, Persien, Holland, Java oder China und wurden jeweils nach ihrem Herkunftsland benannt. Entsprechend ihrer Wesensart und der verwendeten Fertigungstechnik, teilte man sie in unterschiedliche Klassen ein. So kamen zum Beispiel viele Stücke, die mit der Technik des Holz-Block-Druckes oder mit Handzeichnungen gefertigt waren, aus Indien, Persien und China. Aus Java importierte man hauptsächlich SARASA-Stoffe, die mit dem Batik-Verfahren gefärbt waren, holländische und portugiesische Stoffe waren zum größten Teil mit einer Kupferplatten-Drucktechnik gefärbt.

SARASA-Waren, beliebt bei Sammlern und Kennern, zierten meist Muster von Blütenblättern, Gräsern und Tieren wie Vögel, Fische, Insekten. Aber auch Motive wie Puppen, kleine Muster, Ranken, Hieroglyphen oder bildhafte Darstellungen religiöser Szenen oder Erzählungen erfreuten sich großer Beliebtheit. Jedes dieser Ornamente vermittelte etwas vom Volkscharakter oder von den landschaftlichen Eigenheiten seines Herkunftslandes.

Jedesmal wenn die diversen Waren aus Europa, China oder anderen Ländern auf ausländischen Handelsschiffen in den Hafen einliefen, wurde der – nur mit Berechtigungsscheinen zu betretende – Markt für die einge agerten Importwaren geöffnet. Zu eigens festgelegten Zeiten war eine Besichtigung der Lagerware möglich, und es herrschte ein ständiges Kommen und Gehen beschäftigter Europäer und Chinesen, während japanische Staatsdiener, Übersetzer und lizensierte Kaufleute emsig ihre Arbeit verrichteten.

Mit der Öffnung eines von ausländischem Flair stark geprägten Basars ließ sich ein solch lebhaftes Gedränge jedoch auch außerhalb der festgelegten Zeiten täglich auf der Insel Deshima beobachten.

Ursprünglich waren die gemusterten SARASA-Stoffe bunte Baumwolldrucke, aber es gab auch Brokat, chinesische Webware und prächtige, luxeriöse Seidenstoffe einer speziellen Webart. Auf besonderen Wunsch wurden sie mit Stickereien oder Blattgold verziert oder man verwendete auf Bestellung die Muster der importierten SARASA-Ware (WATARI-SARASA).

Bis heute sind viele von Fürsten und Feldherren gern getragene JIMBAORI erhalten geblieben, eine Art Wams, welches über der Rüstung getragen wurde. In der Absicht, den gegenüberstehenden Gegner ohne Worte einzuschüchtern, wurden eigens für die Krieger prächtige und kuriose Muster verwendet, beispielsweise Raubtiere mit mächtigen Körpern, welche die Gegner schon nach einem kurzen Blick zu Boden gehen lassen sollten. Wenn die Krieger ins Schlachtfeld zogen, sollten die Muster und Färbungen der Rüstungen natürlich umso drohender sein. Neben den althergebrachten Namen fanden sich auf den Rüstungen Abbildungen von chinesischen Löwen, Drachen, Tigern oder Monstern, offensichtlich in der Absicht, dem Gegner seine Macht zu demonstrieren.

Als man sich im Lauf der Geschichte ruhigen und friedlichen Zeiten näherte, verschwanden so gewaltige und seltsame Dinge wie die erschreckenden Teufelsmasken. Aber die einfache Stadtbevölkerung, die in einem völlig anderem Milieu als die Fürsten und wohlhabenden Schichten lebte, konnte sich aufgrund ihres tief verwurzelten Sinnes für den Erhalt von Traditionen und ihrem eigenen Begriff von Schönheit noch immer nicht mit den etwas zu lebhaften und exotischen SARASA-Mustern anfreunden. Man beschränkte sich darauf, die als Kleider oder Trachten genutzten SARASA-Textilien auf den Straßen zu bewundern und hegte selbst noch Zweifel in bezug auf das Tragen solcher Kleidungsstücke. Selbst wenn man durch Zufall an ein äußerst seltenes Stück SARASA-Stoffes gelangte, verwendete man es lediglich als Unterkleidung für den Kimono oder fertigte daraus unsichtbare Taschen für die Ärmelaufschläge. SARASA-Textilien aus reiner Seide fanden wiederum ihre Verwendung als Futterstoff für den HAORI, eine Art japanischer Mantel, welcher zu kalten Jahreszeiten über dem Kimono getragen wird.

Aber zum Ende der Tokugawa-Zeit (1853 – 1867) hatte sich auch das einfache Volk mit den SARASA-Mustern vertraut gemacht. Unter der Zusammenarbeit von finanzkräftigen Tuchhändlern, gewinnsüchtigen und neugierigen Großhändlern sowie den neu aufgekommenen Schneidern für westliche Bekleidung entstand nun auch eine neue japanische SARASA-Form, das sogenannte WASARASA. Diese neue Entwicklung verband die Exotik der importierten SARASA-Textilien mit den vertrauten Mustern des traditionellen japanischen YUZENZOME, eine althergebrachte Färbetechnik, bei der man Kleister zum Abdecken der Stoffpartien verwendet.

Aus diesem Grund nannte man das hier als WASARASA Bezeichnete auch „YUZEN-SARASA" oder „SARASA-YUZEN". Vornehmlichster Zweck dieser neuen Textilform war es wohl, zu einem günstigen Preis einen Stoff für die breite Bevölkerungsmasse anbieten zu können. Man befand sich in einem Zeitalter der Reformen, in dem ausländische kulturelle Einflüsse eine wichtige Rolle spielten. So erschien das prächtige und günstig zu erstehende WASARA gerade zu einer Zeit, als die Leute überall nach Neuheiten suchten. Diese neue Modewelle setzte sich von Edo ausgehend über andere Städte bis in die ländlichen Regionen fort und etablierte sich.

Darüber hinaus lebte zum Ende der Edo-Zeit in Kyoto eine Gruppe von Designern, die eine eigene Form des WASARASA herstellten. Dabei handelte es sich um eine prächtige Stoffart, von der es heißt, daß sie die Bedeutung der traditionellen, importierten SARASA-Ware noch übertraf.

Die erwähnten Designer hatten ihr Zentrum in der Gegend um Horikawa/Kyoto und verwendeten in fachmännischer Weise die alte Technik des Schablonenfärbens (KATAZOME). Sie kopierten mit der Zeit fast sämtliche Muster der importierten SARASA-Textilien und schufen somit ein großartiges Werk. Von diesen Mustern gab es mehrere Tausend verschiedene Arten, von denen einige Designer Papierdrucke angefertigt haben sollen, um diese als eine Art Memorandum einzulagern. Leider ist von diesen Mustersammlungen bis heute nur wenig erhalten geblieben. Allerdings spricht man davon, daß diese erhaltenen Muster wieder für neue Arbeiten verwendet werden sollen.

Als die Zeit der Unruhen, die das Ende der Edo-Zeit mit der Meiji-Zeit verbanden, vorüber war, überschwemmte ein Zufluß westlicher Kultur das Land und bewirkte plötzliche Reformen im Alltag der breiten Bevölkerungsmasse. Nach dem Ende der Meijirestauration von 1868 erklang von allen Seiten und Schichten der unaufhörliche Ruf nach einer kulturellen Erneuerung. Dies bewirkte natürlich auch bezüglich der Bekleidung wichtige Veränderungen. Leider neigten nun Männer und Frauen gleichermaßen zum mondänen Lebensstil und interessierten sich für westliche Kleidung. Insbesondere die westliche Mädchenbekleidung umgab ein besonderes Flair, und mit Namen wie „Garderobe für vornehme Damen" verführte man die Leute dazu, solche Neuerungen zu begehren.

Mit dem Erscheinen westlicher Mode war auffälligerweise auch bei WASARASA-Textilien aus reiner Seide eine fortschreitende Entwicklung bemerkbar. Zusammen mit besonders fein bedruckten SARASA-Stoffen aus Baumwolle erfreuten sie sich als Material für westliche Kleidung einer weitreichenden Nachfrage. Sie entsprachen nicht nur dem Stil der Oberschicht, sondern auch dem der einfachen Schichten und färbten zu dieser Zeit der kulturellen Erneuerung Land und Leute. Angefangen von Unterbekleidung für Damen und Herren fertigte man aus diesen Stoffen Dinge des täglichen Gebrauches wie Sonnenschirme, Halstücher, Reisetaschen, Beutel und ähnliches.

Die Lebhaftigkeit, wie man sie während der Meiji-Zeit beispielsweise auf den ständigen Bällen und Banketten sah, wo Mädchen der Oberschicht in Abendgarderoben aus blumenverzierten SARASA-Stoffen Europäern die Hände reichten, um zu tanzen, war noch kurz vorher, zur Zeit des Zerfalls der BAKUFU, undenkbar gewesen und ist sicher als die Wiege der neuen Sitten zu bezeichnen.

Interessant ist hierbei die Überlegung, daß durch den Handelshafen von Deshima/Nagasaki die Aufnahme abendländischer Kultur, Kunst und Wissenschaft ermöglicht wurde. In bezug auf die damals modernen SARASA-Textilien mit importierten Mustern verspüren wir noch heute eine geheimnisvolle Verbundenheit. Diese wird verständlicher, wenn wir uns der Tatsache bewußt werden, daß mit der SARASA-Mode nach 400jähriger Isolation zum zweiten Mal der Vorhang über das Land fiel.

Anfang bis Mitte der Meiji-Zeit verteilten die ländlichen Tuchhändler sowie die Kurz- und Importwarengeschäfte Reklamezettel, auf denen sie Dinge wie westliche SARASA-Textilien, abendländisches Kaliko oder Importkleidung anpriesen. Auch führten sie aus rein seidenen SARASA-Stoffen Kimonos, Untergewänder oder Futterstoffe für den Haori. Baumwollenes YUZEN-SARASA wurde in Form von Tragebeuteln, Futon-Bezügen oder als Stoffe für die Herstellung der Gürtel (OBI) traditioneller japanischer Kleidung angeboten. Egal um welchen ländlichen Bezirk es sich auch handelte, es wurden größtenteils die gleichen Dinge feilgeboten.

Während man, wie bereits vorhin erwähnt, vom Ende der Edo-Zeit bis zur Meiji-Zeit in Horikawa bei Kyoto emsig mit der Fertigung des WASARASA beschäftigt war, wurde in Edo, dem heutigen Tokio, das sogenannte EDO-SARASA hergestellt. Dieses Kunsthandwerk wurde von Meistern des EDO-SARASA ausgeführt, welche besondere Fertigkeiten in der Schablonenfärbetechnik besaßen. Noch heute eben von ihnen einige direkte Nachfahren, die das Erbe der alten SARASA-Meister pflegen und sich glücklicherweise bester Gesundheit erfreuen.

Auch sollte man sich meiner Meinung nach vor Augen halten, daß durch die eigentümliche Technik und die beharrlichen Studien in bezug auf die Eigenart des SARASA viele Kunsthandwerker erhalten geblieben sind – und unabhängig vom sozialen Wandel – in ärmlichen Verhältnissen und mit der Geschichte der ländlichen Eigenheiten leben. Um einige der namhaften Erzeugnisse zu nennen, die nach den Ortsnamen der Gegend, in der sie hergestellt werden, bezeichnet sind, möchte ich Kagoshima-Sarasa, Nagasaki-Sarasa, Sendai-Sarasa, Akita-Sarasa, Edo-Sarasa oder Hirokawa (Kyoto)-Sarasa erwähnen.

Das ebenfalls in diesem Buch behandelte schablonengefärbte SARASA-Papier (Katazome-sarasamoyo-kami) wurde zum größten Teil von einem Kunsthandwerker gesammelt, dessen Familie seit dem Ende der Edo-Zeit in Hirogawa bei Kyoto lebt. Einige seiner Stücke werden heute von der Forschungsgesellschaft für alte Textilien aufbewahrt. Als Ergänzung für die Dokumentation des Wandels der Textilmuster wurde ein Teil dieser Papiere für das vorliegende Buch zusammengestellt und abgebildet. Dieses geschah vor allem mit dem Wunsch, Kunsthandwerkern eine Informationsquelle zu schaffen.

Das erwähnte schablonengefärbte Papier wurde von besonders kunstfertigen Meistern nach einem speziellen Verfahren angefertigt. Dabei wurden mehrere Papierschablonen übereinander gelegt, um ein bestimmtes Druckmuster zu erhalten – oftmals bis zu 20 oder 30 Seiten für ein einziges Muster.

Alle hier abgebildeten Exemplare der Musterblätter stammen aus der Periode ab Ende der Edo- bis Mitte der Meiji-Zeit. Sie waren eine Vorstufe im Druckverfahren für die Textilien und wurden als Testdruck angefertigt. Auch dienten sie den Textildruckern als Aufzeichnungen für spätere Zwecke oder wurden in den Stoffabteilungen größerer Läden als Probeexemplare ausgestellt. Als Schmuckpapier, wie beispielsweise das CHIYOGAMI, wurden sie jedoch so gut wie gar nicht im Handel angeboten.

Dieses Buch will in anschaulicher Weise und so konkret wie möglich einen Überblick über das geschichtliche Erbe der Muster des WATARI-SARASA und des WASARASA geben. In 759 Farbabbildungen wurden die unterschiedlichen Formen und klassischen Motive zusammengestellt. Dieses Buch wurde jedoch nicht zum Zwecke theoretischer Studien publiziert, sondern entstand vielmehr mit dem Wunsch, eine winzige Hilfestellung für all diejenigen zu geben, die durch das Erfassen längst vergessener Werke und Leistungen der alten Meister Neues erschaffen wollen.

Le WASARASA: une brève histoire du WASARASA et du papier SARASA coloré

par Kamon Yoshimoto

Beaucoup d'entre nous ont déjà entendu parler des tissus SARASA. Ce sont des tissus imprimés d'origine japonaise connus aussi sous le nom de WASARASA. (Les Japonais utilisent le préfixe «wa» pour exprimer «Japon, japonais etc..».)

Selon la légende, le «WATARI NO SARASA», qui donna naissance plus tard au SARASA que nous connaissons, transita par les ports hollandais, portugais ou chinois de la fin de l'ère Muromachi jusqu'à l'ère Momoyama ou le début de l'époque Edo (selon d'autres sources, le SARASA remonterait à l'ère Asuka ou Nara).

Une chose est certaine en tout cas: à cette époque, l'importation de SARASA qui se faisait par le port franc de Hirado pour arriver ensuite à Nagasaki/Deshima était florissante tant par la quantité que par la variété des dessins.

Dans les divers registres de commerce de l'époque qui nous renseignent sur les marchandises importées, l'arrivée de tissus SARASA est enregistrée à côté de celle du velours, du calicot, du galon etc... .

Il faut préciser que l'orthographe de SARASA variait beaucoup dans ces documents relatifs à «l'importation de tissus». Ainsi pour la même prononciation existe-t-il diverses orthographes avec deux ou trois caractères chinois ou diverses possibilités de reproduction en katana, le caractère japonais pur. Les interprétations et les thèses sur l'origine des différentes orthographes du mot SARASA ne manquent pas, mais aucune n'est entièrement satisfaisante. Voici quelques-unes des thèses avancées:

1. Le mot sarasa désigne un lieu en Inde.
2. Le mot est d'origine hollandaise.
3. L'appellation serait originaire du Portugal.
4. SARASA est un mot d'un dialecte du sud du Japon.
5. Il s'agit de tissus imprimés de l'empire des Sarasènes.

Nombre de ces théories viennent d'anciens philosophes et érudits mais on ne peut les considérer comme définitives. La seule thèse qui met tout le monde d'accord est qu'il n'y a aucune théorie à valeur générale, aussi a-t-on tendance à parler d'un mystère des étoffes.

Depuis peu certaines personnes prétendent que SARASA est un terme technique international, soit étranger soit purement japonais, désignant un motif. Si l'on demande à des visiteurs du Japon qui n'y font qu'un bref séjour ce que signifie le terme japonais SARASA ou l'expression Sarasatic pattern, on n'obtient aucune réponse, sauf de la part d'étrangers vivant dans le pays depuis longtemps. Cela s'explique par le fait que ce que les Japonais désignent avec le mot SARASA porte à l'étranger les noms les plus divers. Ainsi parle-t-on de Printed textiles, printed cotton textiles, indienne ou calico painting, en Indonésie on parle de batik et les Britanniques disent chintz.

Les nouveaux motifs SARASA des Européens et des Chinois surprirent les Japonais par leur somptuosité et leur coloris curieux, si libre et si désinvolte, et amenèrent des changements dans de nombreux domaines. Ces changements se manifestèrent dans la conception des ornements qui étaient jusque-là imprégnés de la sensibilité japonaise, des designs et des motifs de vêtements, sans oublier les représentations métaphoriques de fleurs et d'oiseaux ou la manière traditionnelle réaliste avec laquelle on représentait l'harmonie de la nature et du paysage.

Mais un réveil s'opéra aussi dans la tournure d'esprit japonaise dont il est généralement difficile de se défaire. D'une certaine manière on peut dire que ce textile importé était un vent frais soufflant dans le monde vieillissant des motifs colorés japonais. Il a apporté également, comme on a pu le constater, un élément de douceur dans les motifs ultérieurs de la mousseline et les kosode (kimonos en tissu ouatiné).

D'un seul coup les tissus SARASA étaient promus au rang d'article de mode à admirer et désirer. En raison de leur prix élevé seuls les princes (daimyo), les nobles, les chevaliers de haut rang et les riches commerçants pouvaient les acheter, pour les gens du peuple ils étaient carrément inabordables. De plus, n'étant portés qu'à certaines occasions comme vêtement luxueux ou comme parure pour la cérémonie du thé, ils se trouvaient entre les mains de familles de samurai célèbres et de maîtres de cérémonie du thé. En raison de leur prix élevé ils restaient inaccessibles au peuple autant qu'une fleur au sommet de la plus haute montagne.

Les différents tissus SARASA importés (WATARI-SARASA) venaient à l'époque d'Inde, du Siam, de Perse, de Hollande, de Java ou de Chine et étaient appelés selon leur pays d'origine. Ils étaient classés par genre et par technique de fabrication. De nombreux tissus imprimés, par exemple avec une matrice de bois ou des dessins faits à la main, arrivaient d'Inde, de Perse et de Chine. De Java on importait essentiellement des tissus SARASA teints selon le procédé du batik; les étoffes hollandaises et portugaises étaient en majeure partie teintes selon un procédé d'impression sur planche de cuivre.

Les tissus SARASA tels que les collectionneurs et les connaisseurs les aimaient étaient décorés pour la plupart de motifs de pétales de fleurs, de graminées et d'animaux comme les oiseaux, les poissons, les insectes.

Mais d'autres motifs décoraient aussi ces tissus comme les poupées, petits dessins, vrilles, hiéroglyphes ou représentations métaphoriques de scènes religieuses ou de récits qui étaient toujours très appréciés. Chacun de ces ornements reproduisait un fragment du caractère et de la particularité des paysages de son pays d'origine.

Chaque fois qu'un navire marchand en provenance d'Europe, de Chine ou d'autres contrées entrait dans un port japonais, l'entrepôt des marchandises importées s'ouvrait à tout porteur d'une autorisation spéciale. On ouvrait à certaines heures et il y avait à ce moment-là un va-et-vient permanent d'Européens et de Chinois très occupés tandis que des fonctionnaires japonais, des traducteurs et des commerçants licenciés s'affairaient à leur travail.

Mais la bousculade dans ce marché à l'européenne ne se limitait pas aux heures d'ouverture, chaque jour on pouvait observer la même activité fébrile sur l'île de Deshima.

Les premiers tissus SARASA imprimés étaient des cotons colorés mais il y avait aussi du brocart, des étoffes de Chine et des soieries au tissage spécial splendides et luxueuses. Sur demande il était possible de les faire broder ou décorer avec de l'or en feuilles ou même d'utiliser sur commande les motifs de la marchandise SARASA importée (WATARI-SARASA).

Nous avons pu conserver de très vieux Jimbaori, une sorte de pourpoint que les princes et les généraux portaient sur leur cuirasse. Dans le but d'impressionner leur adversaire sans prononcer le moindre mot, les guerriers avaient recours à des motifs extraordinaires et curieux, par exemple des fauves au corps puissant dont la seule vue devait remplir l'ennemi d'effroi.

Les motifs et les couleurs de l'armure devaient paraître encore plus menaçants lorsque les guerriers partaient sur le champ de bataille. Le nom du guerrier côtoyait alors des lions chinois, des dragons ou des monstres qui avaient pour fonction de montrer sa force et son pouvoir à l'adversaire.

La paix revenant, ce qui symbolisait encore la violence comme les masques diaboliques commençait à être superflu et finit par disparaître. Mais la population des villes ne se faisait toujours pas aux motifs SARASA joyeux et exotiques: vivant dans un tout autre milieu que les princes et les riches, elle restait profondément attachée aux traditions et à sa propre conception de la beauté. Elle se contentait donc d'admirer dans la rue les tissus SARASA sous la forme de vêtements ou costumes à la mode et se demandait comment on pouvait porter des choses pareilles.

Même si par hasard elle entrait en possession d'un morceau de tissu SARASA très rare, elle s'en servait comme vêtement de dessous ou confectionnait des poches pour les revers de manches. Par contre les étoffes SARASA en soie pure étaient utilisées comme doublure de haori, une sorte de manteau japonais porté sur le kimono pendant la saison froide.

Vers la fin de l'époque Tokugawa (1853–1867) les gens du peuple s'étaient enfin habitués aux motifs SARASA. Sous l'influence de drapiers puissants, de négociants curieux et avides au gain, ainsi que de tailleurs spécialisés dans la mode occidentale, une nouvelle forme japonaise de SARASA avait vu le jour, le WASARASA.

Il constituait la synthèse de l'exotisme des tissus SARASA importés et des motifs du YUZENZOME traditionnel (très ancienne technique de teinture consistant à couvrir les parties du tissu avec de la colle). Ainsi ce tissu que l'on désigne sous le nom de WASARASA est-il appelé aussi «YUZEN-SARASA» ou «SARASA-YUZEN». L'objectif premier de ce nouveau textile était de mettre un tissu bon marché à la disposition de la majeure partie de la population. On était en pleine époque de réformes portant l'empreinte de la culture occidentale. Le WASARA superbe et bon marché apparaissait justement au moment où les gens recherchaient la nouveauté. Partie d'Edo, la mode s'élança à l'assaut des autres villes puis des régions campagnardes avant de s'installer pour longtemps dans le pays.

A la fin de l'époque Edo, un groupe de stylistes installés à Kyoto développa sa propre forme de WASARA. Il s'agissait d'une étoffe magnifique dont l'importance dépassait celle du tissu SARASA traditionnel importé.

Les stylistes en question, qui avaient leur centre dans la région de Horikawa/ Kyoto, utilisaient l'ancienne technique de l'impression au pochoir (Katazome). Ils finirent par copier tous les motifs des textiles SARASA importés et créèrent ainsi une œuvre extraordinaire. Il existait quelques milliers de ces motifs que certains stylistes auraient imprimés sur papier, paraît-il, pour en faire un mémorandum. Malheureusement il ne nous est pas resté grand-chose de ces collections. On raconte cependant que le peu qui put être conservé a été réutilisé pour de nouveaux travaux.

Après la période de troubles qui marqua la transition entre l'époque Edo et l'ère Meiji, un flot de culture occidentale inonda le pays et fut à l'origine de réformes assez soudaines dans la vie quotidienne de la population. La période de restauration Meiji terminée, un désir de renouveau culturel se fit sentir de tous côtés et dans tous les milieux sociaux. Ce ne fut pas sans conséquences sur l'habillement.

Hommes et femmes avaient maintenant la fâcheuse tendance à adopter un style de vie mondain et à s'intéresser à la mode occidentale. Spécialement la mode européenne pour les jeunes filles était réputée et des noms comme «garde-robe pour dames distinguées» avaient un grand pouvoir de suggestion sur les gens.

Avec l'apparition de la mode occidentale les textiles WASARASA en soie naturelle connurent un développement spectaculaire. Ils constituaient avec les tissus SARASA de coton très finement imprimés le matériau de l'habillement occidental et étaient de plus en plus recherchés. Ils ne correspondaient pas seulement au style de la classe dominante mais aussi à celui des gens du peuple et déteignaient, dans cette phase de renouveau culturel, sur le pays et la population. Mis à part la lingerie masculine et féminine, ces nouveaux textiles servaient à confectionner des objets de la vie courante tels parasols, foulards, sacs de voyage, bourses et bien d'autres choses encore.

Peu de temps avant, à l'époque du déclin des BAKUFU, il aurait été inimaginable de voir, comme c'était le cas à l'ère Meiji, une jeune fille de la bonne société avec une robe confectionnée dans une étoffe SARASA imprimée à fleurs tendre sa fine main à un Européen qui l'invitait à danser, et on peut considérer à juste titre ce dynamisme comme le berceau de nouvelles coutumes.

Il est intéressant à ce propos de noter que la diffusion de la culture, de l'art et de la science du vieux monde se soit faite par le port de commerce de Deshima/ Nagasaki. Nous sentons encore en nous un attachement mystérieux pour ces étoffes SARASA aux motifs importés si modernes à l'époque, attachement qui est dû au fait que nous savons qu'avec la mode SARASA le rideau tombe pour la seconde fois sur le pays après 400 ans d'isolation.

Du début jusqu'au milieu de l'ère Meiji, les drapiers ruraux ainsi que les merciers et les importateurs distribuaient des réclames où ils vantaient la beauté et la qualité des étoffes SARASA occidentales, du calicot européen ou des vêtements d'importation. Ils vendaient aussi des soieries SARASA pour les kimonos, pour les vêtements de dessous et les doublures de haori. Les cotonnades YUZEN-SARASA étaient destinées aux bourses, aux enveloppes de futton ou présentées comme tissus dans lesquels étaient confectionnées les ceintures (obi) des vêtements traditionnels japonais. Peu importe la région, les marchands proposaient toujours les mêmes choses.

De la fin de l'époque Edo à l'ère Meiji, tandis que, comme on l'a déjà évoqué, on fabriquait le WASARA à Horikawa près de Kyoto, on fabriquait le tissu dit EDO-SARASA à Edo. Cet artisanat était exécuté par des maîtres qui avaient acquis un grand savoir-faire dans le domaine de la teinture au pochoir. Ils ont eu des successeurs dont certains vivent encore − et Dieu merci en bonne santé − dans le respect de l'héritage des anciens maîtres SARASA.

Il ne faut pas perdre de vue le fait que grâce à la technique particulière et la recherche opiniâtre liées à la nature même du SARASA il existe encore beaucoup d'artisans-artistes SARASA qui vivent − indépendamment des mutations sociales − dans des conditions misérables, entourés de l'histoire des traditions rurales. Parmi les étoffes Sarasa connues mentionnons le Kagoshima-Sarasa, le Nagasaki-Sarasa, le Sendai-Sarasa, l'Akita-Sarasa, l'Edo-Sarasa ou le Hirokawa (Kyoto)-Sarasa.

Nous avons déjà évoqué dans ce livre le papier SARASA (Katazome-sarasamoyo-kami) imprimé au pochoir. Un artisan d'art, dont la famille vit à Hirogawa près de Kyoto depuis la fin de l'ère Edo, collectionna une grande partie de ce papier. Quelques-unes de ses pièces de collection sont conservées aujourd'hui par la Société de recherche sur les textiles anciens. Pour compléter la documentation sur l'histoire de ces motifs, une partie de ces spécimens a été tout spécialement réunie et reproduite dans ce livre, l'intention première étant de fournir une source d'information aux artisans d'art.

Le papier SARASA était fabriqué par des artisans accomplis selon un procédé spécial: plusieurs découpes, parfois jusqu'à 20 ou 30, étaient posées l'une sur l'autre pour obtenir le motif désiré.

Tous les exemplaires ici exposés datent de la fin de l'époque Edo jusqu'au milieu de l'ère Meiji. Ils constituaient le stade préliminaire de la teinture et étaient fabriqués pour les essais d'impression. Ils servaient de dessins aux artisans dans le cadre d'autres travaux ou ils étaient exposés comme échantillons aux rayons tissus des grandes boutiques. En revanche on les trouvait rarement dans le commerce sous forme de papier décoratif tel que le CHIYOGAMI.

Donner une vue d'ensemble claire et concrète de l'héritage historique des motifs WATARI-SARASA et WASARASA, tel est le but de ce livre. Les 759 illustrations permettent de découvrir les diverses formes et les motifs de ces ornements. Ce livre n'a pas été publié en vue d'études théoriques, il est né de l'idée d'aider en toute modestie tous ceux qui désirent créer du nouveau par la compréhension d'œuvres oubliées depuis longtemps et liées au travail des maîtres d'antan.

KATAZOME – Sample test-prints on paper (original)
KATAZOME – Muster-Probedrucke auf Papier (Originale)
KATAZOME – Epreuves de motifs sur papier

KATAZOME paper was manufactured according to a special process that required great skill and subtlety on the part of the master or artisan producing it. To create each of these papers, two to ten cut-stencil pages were laid on top of each other before the dyeing was performed. In a few exceptional cases, twenty to thirty and sometimes even more paper stencils were employed.

KATAZOME-Papier wurde nach einem speziellen Verfahren hergestellt, das von den Druckmeistern eine besondere Kunstfertigkeit verlangte. Für die Fertigung jedes dieser Papiere legte man zwei bis zehn Blätter eines Schnittmuster-Papieres übereinander und bedruckte sie. Darüber hinaus existieren auch Werke, bei denen man für ein einziges Muster zwanzig bis dreißig oder sogar mehr Papier-Schablonen verwendete.

Le papier KATAZOME était fabriqué selon un procédé spécial au pochoir qui exigeait des artisans un grand savoir-faire. Il fallait de deux à dix découpes de papier fin posées une à une pour réaliser l'impression mais certains motifs en nécessitaient de vingt à trente, parfois même plus.

拾參枚型

九枚型

拾參枚型

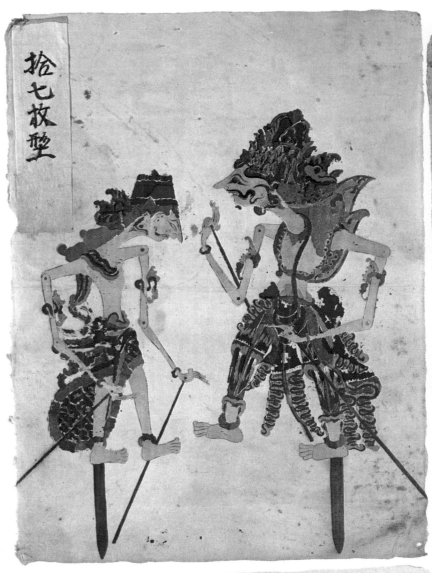

拾
七
枚
型

拾
六
枚
型

七
枚
型

貳枚型

KATAZOME – Display palettes for textile prints (original)
KATAZOME – Schaupaletten für Textildrucke (Originale)
KATAZOME – Planches de démonstration pour motifs de textiles (originaux)

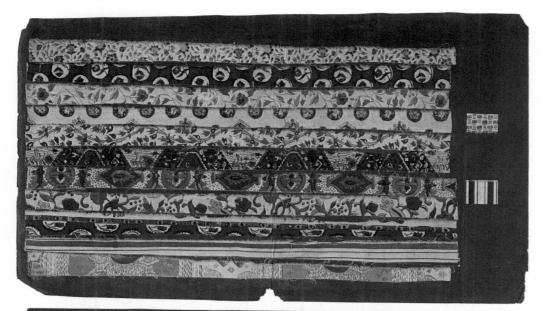

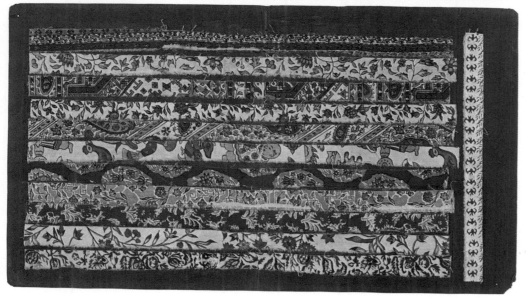

These display palettes were used as sample books in cloth stores and colour presses during the Edo period and up until the beginning of Meiji times.

Diese Schaupaletten wurden ab der Edo-Zeit bis zu den Anfangsjahren der Meiji-Zeit in Stoffläden und Färbereien als Musterbücher verwendet.

Ces planches de démonstration furent exposées de l'époque Edo jusqu'au début de l'ère Meiji dans les échoppes de drapiers et chez les teinturiers.

Patterned Textiles – Examples of their uses (original)
Gemusterte Textilien – Verwendungsbeispiele (Originale)
Textiles imprimés – Exemples d'utilisation (originaux)

Part of a doll's kimono
from the late Edo period, with KOMON pattern
(minutest of patterns, produced with stencils and traces of paste).
Teil eines Puppenkimonos
aus der späten Edo-Zeit mit Komon-Muster
(kleinteiligste, mit Schablonen und Kleister erzeugte Musterung).
Fragment d'un kimono de poupée
de la fin de l'époque Edo dans un motif Komon (petits motifs imprimés au
pochoir et colle de réserve).

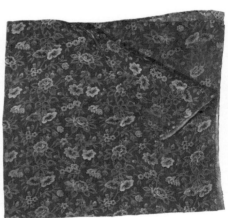

Purse set (oyako komonoire)
Purse set with WATARI pattern from
the end of the Edo period.
Taschenset (oyako komonoire)
Taschenset mit WATARI-Muster aus
dem Ende der Edo-Zeit.
Set de pochettes (oyako komonoire)
Set de pochettes imprimées d'un motif
WATARI de la fin de de l'époque Edo.

Carrier shawl (furushiki)
With floral pattern, from
the end of the Edo period.
Tragetuch (furushiki)
mit Blumenmuster aus dem
Ende der Edo-Zeit.
**Châle porte-bébé
(furushiki)**
dans un imprimé fleuri de
la fin de l'époque Edo.

Old Japanese buckle shoe (tabi)
Arabesque with flowers
dating from the middle of the Meiji period.
Altjapanische Schnallensocken (tabi)
Arabeske mit Blumen
aus der Mitte der Meiji-Zeit.
Anciennes chaussettes-boucles (tabi)
Arabesque et fleurs
du milieu de l'ère Meiji.

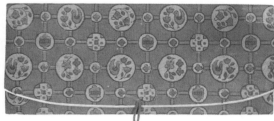

Wallet (fumibasami)
Small cloth wallet of the kind used at the end of the Edo period to
keep documents and letters. Here with bird and floral patterns.
Brieftasche (fumibasami)
Kleine Stofftasche, welche zum Ende der Edo-Zeit für die Aufbe-
wahrung von Dokumenten und Briefen verwendet wurde. Hier
mit einem Vogel- und Blumen-Muster.
Portefeuille (fumibasami)
Pochette en tissu pour la conservation de documents et de
lettres. Ici dans un motif à oiseaux et à fleurs.

Book binding
Binding of the book
"Akoroshi" by Jiro Osaragi,
published in 1929.
Edgings of SOSAKU SARASA.
Bucheinband
Einband des Buches
„Akoroshi" von Jiro Osaragi,
erschienen im Jahr 1929.
Verziert mit SOSAKU-SARASA.
Reliure de livre
Reliure du livre «Akoroshi»
de Jiro Osaragi paru en 1929.
Décoré de SOSAKU-SARASA.

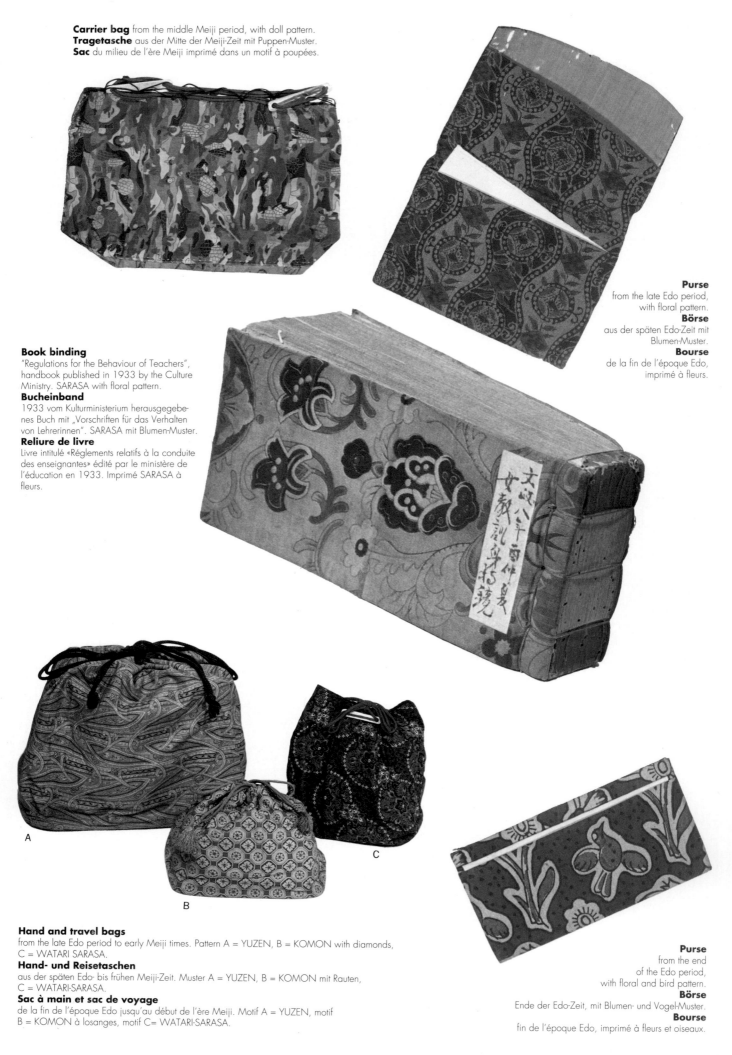

Carrier bag from the middle Meiji period, with doll pattern.
Tragetasche aus der Mitte der Meiji-Zeit mit Puppen-Muster.
Sac du milieu de l'ère Meiji imprimé dans un motif à poupées.

Purse
from the late Edo period,
with floral pattern.
Börse
aus der späten Edo-Zeit mit
Blumen-Muster.
Bourse
de la fin de l'époque Edo,
imprimé à fleurs.

Book binding
"Regulations for the Behaviour of Teachers",
handbook published in 1933 by the Culture
Ministry. SARASA with floral pattern.
Bucheinband
1933 vom Kulturministerium herausgegebe-
nes Buch mit „Vorschriften für das Verhalten
von Lehrerinnen". SARASA mit Blumen-Muster.
Reliure de livre
Livre intitulé «Réglements relatifs à la conduite
des enseignantes» édité par le ministère de
l'éducation en 1933. Imprimé SARASA à
fleurs.

A

B

C

Hand and travel bags
from the late Edo period to early Meiji times. Pattern A = YUZEN, B = KOMON with diamonds,
C = WATARI SARASA.
Hand- und Reisetaschen
aus der späten Edo- bis frühen Meiji-Zeit. Muster A = YUZEN, B = KOMON mit Rauten,
C = WATARI-SARASA.
Sac à main et sac de voyage
de la fin de l'époque Edo jusqu'au début de l'ère Meiji. Motif A = YUZEN, motif
B = KOMON à losanges, motif C= WATARI-SARASA.

Purse
from the end
of the Edo period,
with floral and bird pattern.
Börse
Ende der Edo-Zeit, mit Blumen- und Vogel-Muster.
Bourse
fin de l'époque Edo, imprimé à fleurs et oiseaux.

WASARASA
Patterns with plants in bloom

WASARASA
Muster mit blühenden Pflanzen

WASARASA
Motifs floraux

The SARASA patterns most often encountered depict plants in full bloom. There are patterns with buds, leaves, reeds and trees as the main motifs. As well as compositions using both flowers and reeds, there are also patterns which use only reeds or only flowers. Beyond this there are countless variations of arabesques formed from stalks, tendrils, or leaves.

Generally speaking, whole flowers are used in the larger patterns, leaves of flowers form the average-sized patterns, and tiny details of flowers are used for the most subtle patterns. In recent years nearly half of all ladies' clothing has been edged with the patterns of plants in bloom.

The most often-used Japanese motifs are chrysanthemums, maples, lilies, willows, pomegranate trees, ginger, arabesques, sesame, and giant peonies.

The foreign motifs most often encountered are roses, hyacinths, tulips, Cosmos bipinnatus, sunflowers, and cypresses.

Blühende Pflanzen sind die am häufigsten verwendeten Muster des SARASA. So gibt es beispielsweise Muster mit Blüten, Blättern, Gräsern oder Bäumen. Neben Kompositionen aus Blumen und Gräsern existieren auch Muster, die entweder nur aus Gräsern oder aus Blumen bestehen. Darüber hinaus gibt es in unzähligen Varianten Arabesken aus Halmen, Ranken oder Blättern.

Generell gesagt verwendet man bei großen Mustern Blumen als Motiv, bei mittleren Blütenblätter und bei kleineren Mustern kleinteilige Blumensorten. In den letzten Jahren zierten etwa die Hälfte aller Damenbekleidungen Muster mit blühenden Pflanzen.

Die häufigsten Motive Japans sind: Chrysanthemen, Ahorn, Lilie, Weide, Granatapfelbaum, Zingi-Ingwer, Arabesken, Sesam, Riesenpäonie.

Die häufigsten ausländischen Motive: Rose, Hyazinthe, Tulpe, Schmuckkörbchen (Cosmos bipinnatus), Sonnenblume, Zypresse.

Les plantes en pleine floraison sont un motif récurrent du SARASA. Les motifs de fleurs, d'herbes ou d'arbres sont ceux qui reviennent le plus. Outre les compositions de fleurs et de graminées on trouve d'autres motifs constitués uniquement de graminées ou de fleurs. Il existe aussi de très nombreuses variantes d'arabesques à feuilles, paille ou vrille.

On peut dire qu'en général les grands motifs sont à fleurs, les moyens à feuilles et les autres à petites fleurs. Au cours des dernières années, la moitié à peu près des vêtements féminins étaient ornés de plantes en pleine floraison.

Les motifs japonais les plus fréquents sont: les chrysanthèmes, l'érable, le lys, le saule, le grenadier, le gingembre Zingi, les arabesques, le sésame et la grande pivoine.

Les motifs étrangers les plus fréquents sont: la rose, la jacinthe, la tulipe, le tournesol, le cyprès.

1

2

3

4

5

6

7

8

9

10

11

12

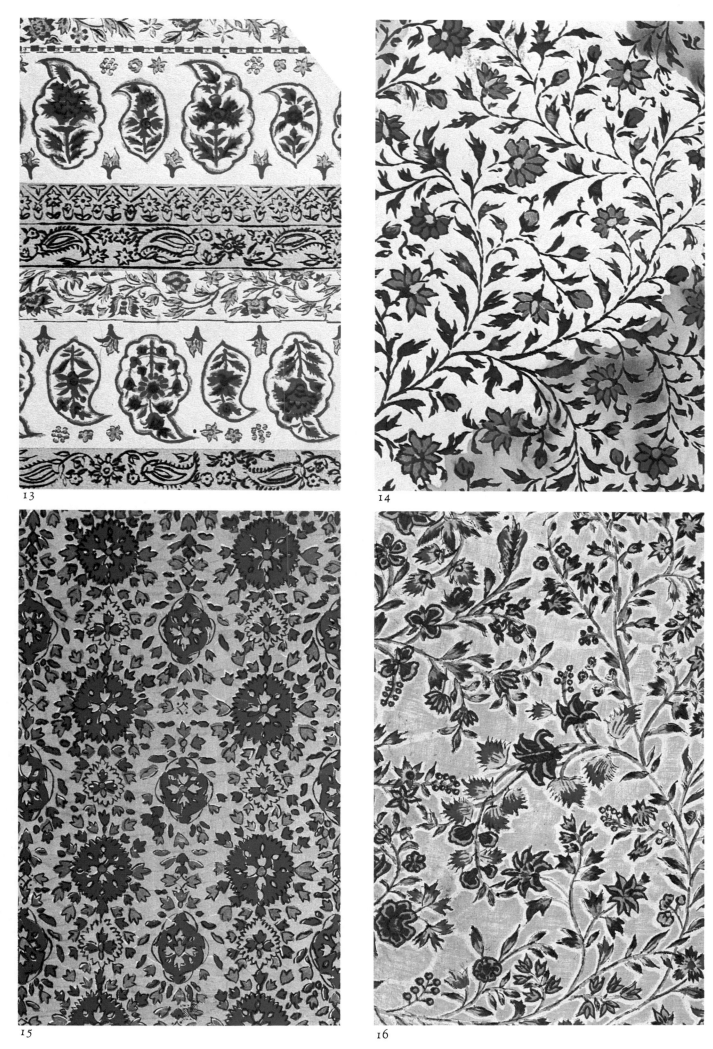

13

14

15

16

17

18

19

20

21

22

23

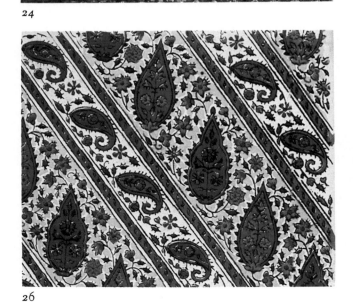

24

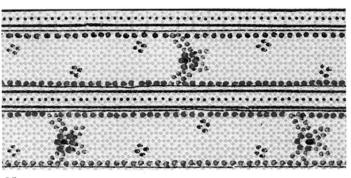

25

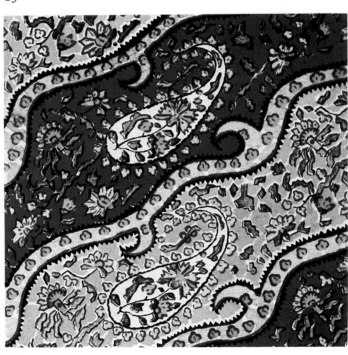

26

27

28

29

30

31

32

33

34

35

36

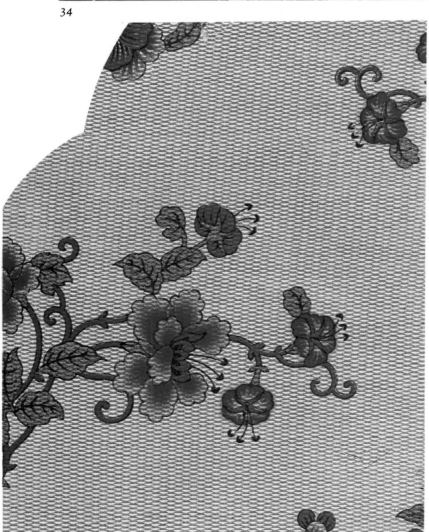

37

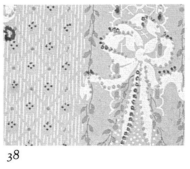

38

39

40

41

42

43

44

45

46

47

48

49

50

51

52

53

54

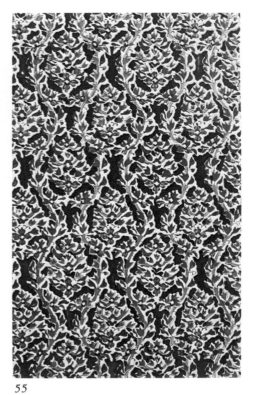

55

56

57

58

59

60

61

62

63

64

65

66

67

68

69

70

71

72

73

74

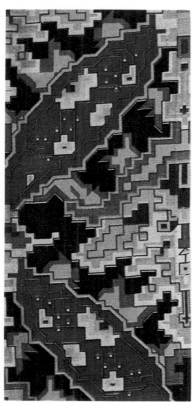

75

76

77

78

79

80

KOMON Patterns

KOMON-Muster

Motifs KOMON

Small and dainty patterns are so typical for Japan that one thinks immediately of the EDO KOMON the very moment that subtly-patterned textiles are even mentioned. Compared to other subtle and refined ornamentation, SARASA KOMON shines with pronounced coloration and exotic patterns incorporating exceptional elegance and natural lines.

For years it has enjoyed constant popularity among the Japanese and can be seen decorating ladies' dresses and men's shirts in all seasons of the year.

The most often-encountered Japanese motifs are oxalis, strawberries, poppies, ginseng leaves, cherry blossom, circular and spiral patterns (TOMOE), horsetail, arabesques, salt and pepper, bamboo, cloisonné, plum blossom, windmills, hemp.

The most often-encountered foreign motifs are subtle flower patterns from Persia and Indonesia, small roses, Cosmos bipinnatus.

Kleine und zierliche Muster sind für Japan so typisch, daß man gleich an das sogenannte EDO-KOMON denkt, wenn man von kleingemusterten Textilien spricht. Im Vergleich zu anderen kleinen Mustern, strahlt das SARASA-KOMON mit seiner prächtigen Färbung und seinen exotischen Formen eine besondere Eleganz und Natürlichkeit aus.

Seit Jahren erfreut es sich bei den Japanern einer kontinuierlichen Beliebtheit und schmückt zu allen Jahreszeiten Damenbekleidung und Herrenhemden.

Die häufigsten Motive Japans: Sauerklee, Erdbeere, Mohn, Gingkoblätter, Kirschblüten, kreis- und wirbelförmige Muster (TOMOE), Schachtelhalm, Arabesken, Pfeffer und Salz, Bambus, Cloisonne-Designs, Pflaumenblüten, Windräder, Hanf.

Die häufigsten ausländischen Motive: kleinförmige Blumenmuster aus Persien und Indonesien, kleine Rosen, Schmuckkörbchen (Cosmos bipinnatus).

Les motifs petits et gracieux sont tellement typiques du Japon que l'on pense tout de suite au EDO-KOMON quand on parle de textiles aux dessins réduits. Par rapport à d'autres dessins de petite taille, le SARASA-KOMON dégage une élégance particulière avec ses coloris éclatants et ses motifs exotiques.

Depuis plusieurs années, il est apprécié sans discontinuer des Japonais et décore en toutes saisons les habits des femmes et les chemises des hommes.

Motifs japonais les plus fréquents: oxalide, fraises, coquelicots, feuilles de ginseng, fleurs de cerisier, motifs de cercles et de spirales (TOMOE), prêle, arabesques, poivre et sel, bambous, cloisonnés, fleurs de prunier, moulins, chanvre.

Motifs étrangers les plus fréquents: petits dessins de fleurs originaires de Perse et d'Indonésie, petites roses, cosméas doubles (Cosmos bipinnatus).

1

2

3

4

5

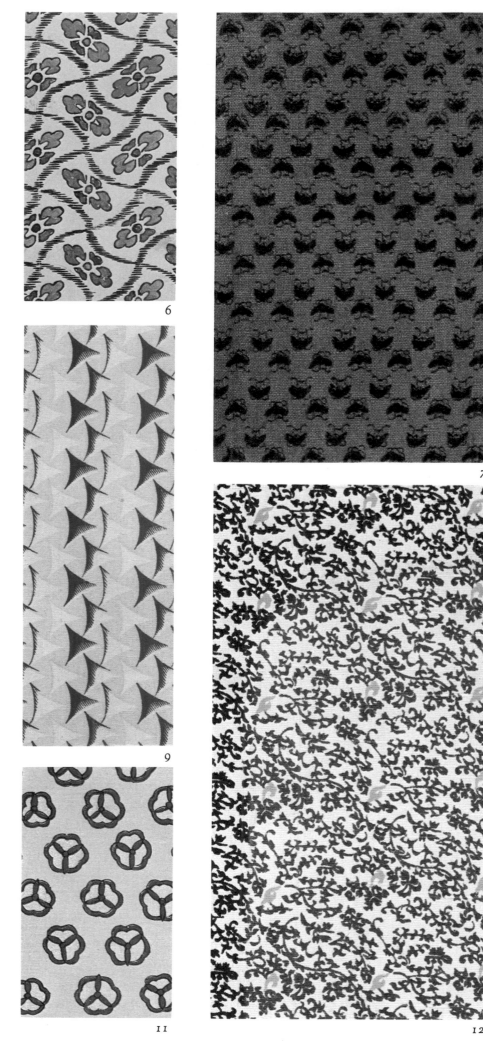

6

7

8

9

10

11

12

13

14

17

15

16

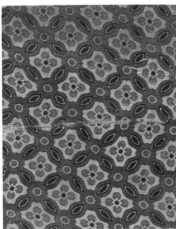

18

19

20

21

22

23

24

27

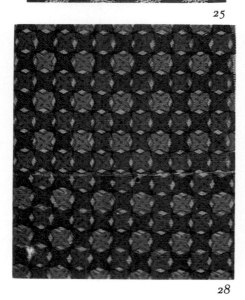

25

26

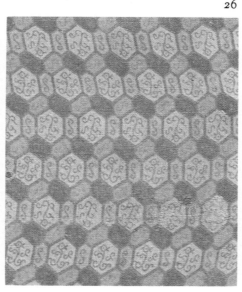

28

29

30

31

32

33

34

35

36

37

38

39

40

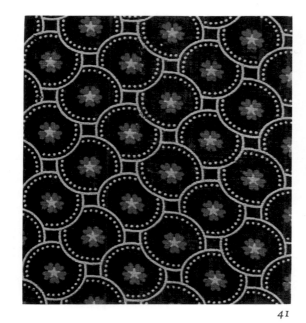

41

42

44

45

46

47

48

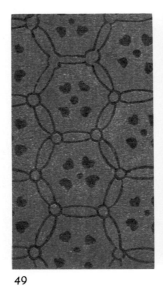
49

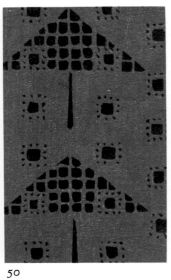
50

51

52

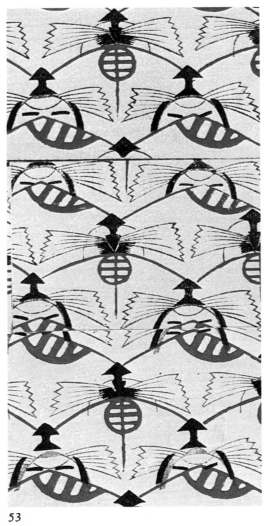
53

54

55

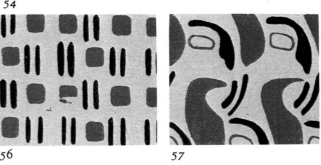
56 57

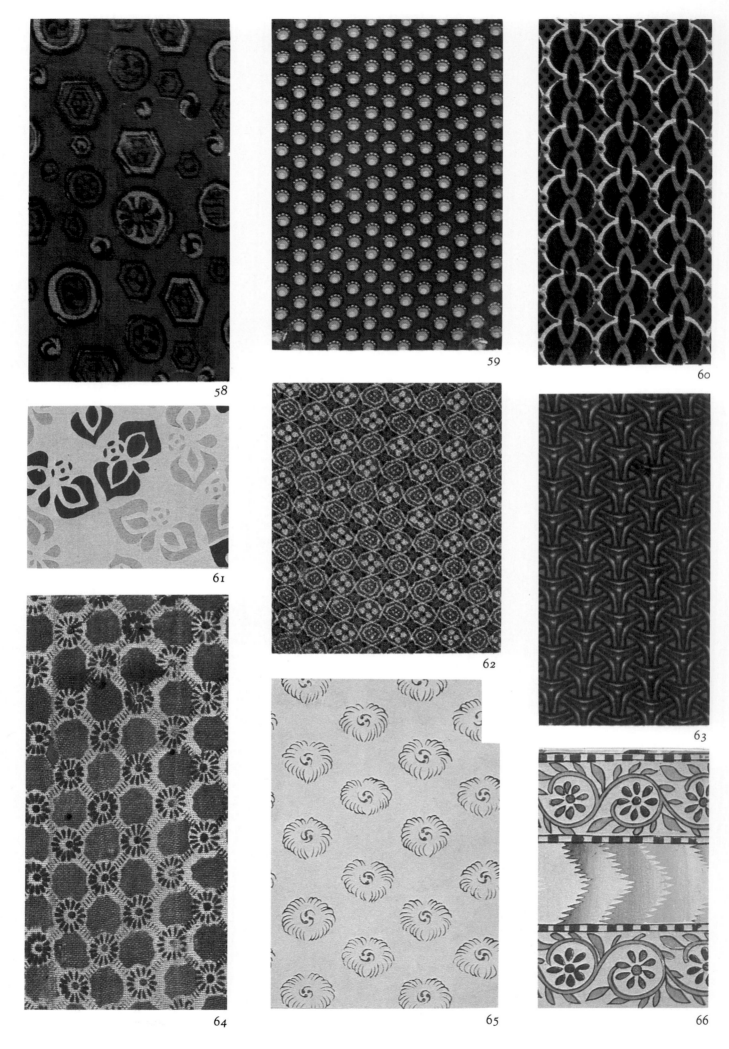

58

59

60

61

62

63

64

65

66

67

68

69

70

71

72

73

74

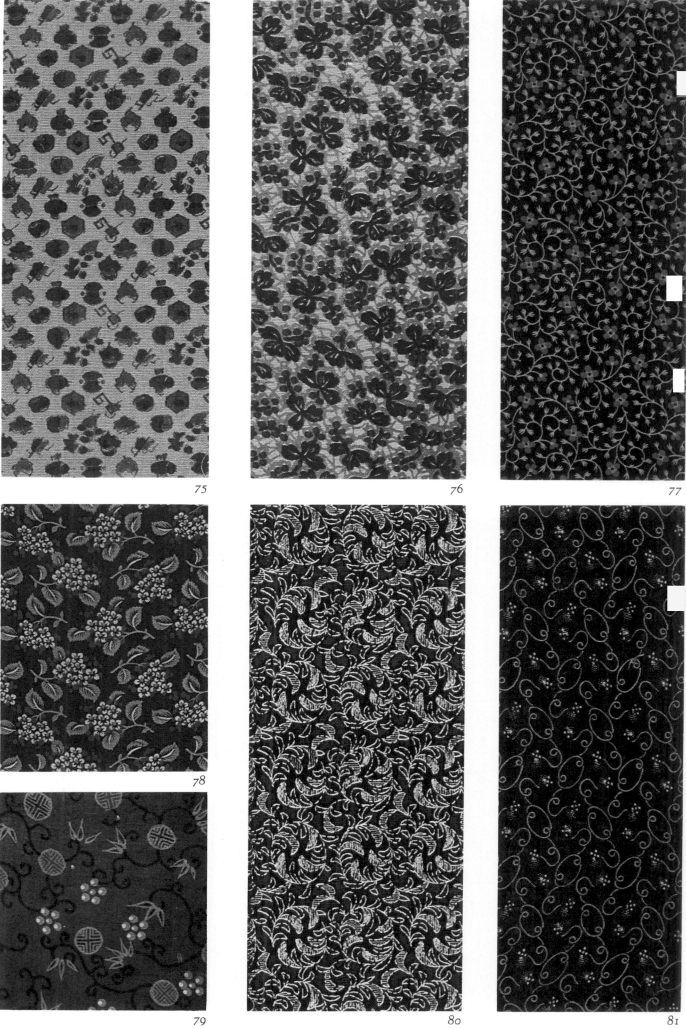

75

76

77

78

79

80

81

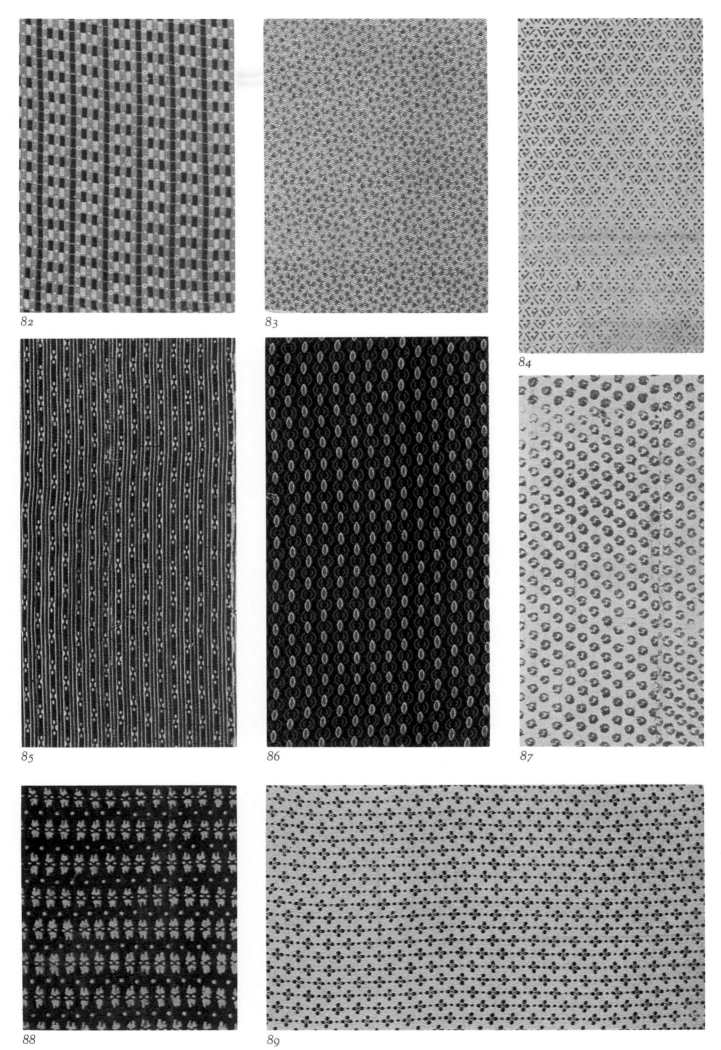

82

83

84

85

86

87

88

89

51

90

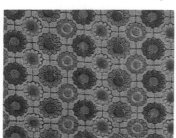

91

92

93

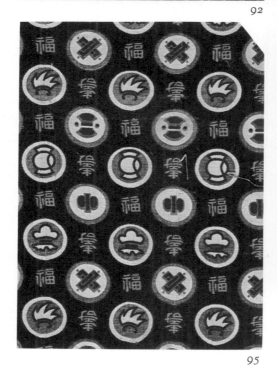

94

95

96

97

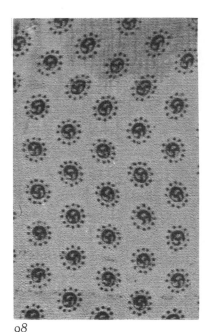

98

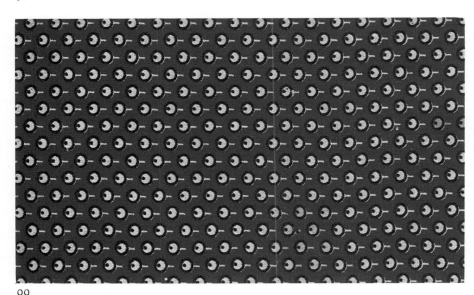

99

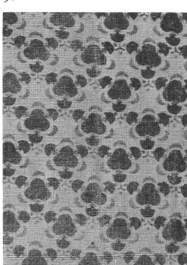

100

101

102

103

104

105

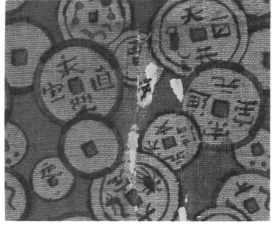

106

107

108

109

110

111

112

113

114

115

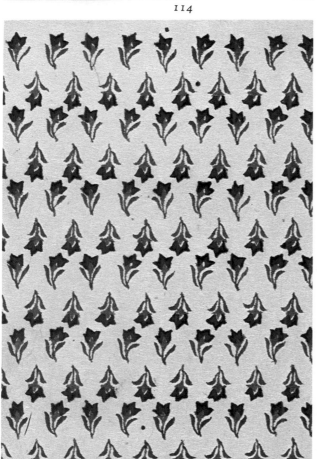

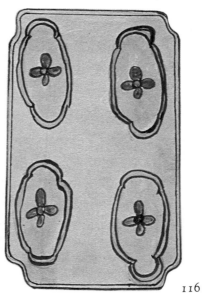

116

117

118

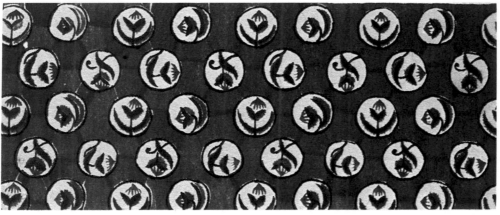

119

YUZEN WASARASA Patterns

YUZEN-WASARASA-Muster

Motifs YUZEN-WASARASA

WATARI SARASA (SARASA introduced by foreigners) was very expensive and simply too exotic and strange for common folk.

For this reason there eventually arose WASARASA, a form which mixed elements of WATARI SARASA and the traditional YUZEN. Under various names like YUZEN SARASA or SARASA YUZEN, the form spread out from EDO (TOKYO) throughout the country to remote regions and fishing villages, where it was employed for kimonos, futon upholstery, carryalls and various small objects.

The Japanese motifs most often encountered are open and closed fans, two interlocking circles, pine, bamboo, plum tree, maple, horsetail, chrysanthemum, poppies, large arabesques, pillows, rising steam.

The foreign motif most often encountered is medium-sized melon trees.

WATARI-SARASA (von den Ausländern eingeführtes SARASA) war sehr kostspielig und für die einfache Bevölkerung zu exotisch und kurios.

Aus diesem Grund entstand im Laufe der Zeit eine Mischform aus WATARI-SARASA und dem traditionellen YUZEN, das WASARASA. Unter verschiedenen Bezeichnungen wie YUZEN-SARASA oder SARASA-YUZEN verbreitete es sich von EDO (TOKIO) ausgehend bis in die ländlichen Regionen und Fischerdörfer, wo es für Kimonos, Futon-Bezüge, Taschen und kleine Gebrauchsgegenstände verwendet wurde.

Häufigste Motive Japans: geöffnete und geschlossene Fächer, zwei in sich verschlungene Kreise, Kiefer, Bambus, Pflaumenbaum, Ahorn, Schachtelhalm, Chrysantheme, Mohn, große Arabesken, Kissen, aufsteigender Dampf.

Das häufigste ausländische Motiv: mittelgroßer Melonenbaum.

Le WATARI-SARASA (importé de l'étranger) était très coûteux et pour les gens du peuple trop exotique et curieux.

C'est la raison qui explique l'apparition progressive d'un composé constitué du WATARI-SARASA et du traditionnel YUZEN, le WASARASA. Sous des appellations différentes telles YUZEN-SARASA ou SARASA-YUZEN, il se répandit de la capitale EDO (TOKYO) jusque dans les régions et les villages de pêcheurs les plus reculés du Japon où on l'utilisa pour les kimonos, les enveloppes de futton, les sacs et les menus objets.

Les motifs japonais les plus fréquents sont: les éventails fermés et ouverts, deux cercles entrelacés, le pin, le bambou, le prunier, l'érable, la prêle, le chrysanthème, le pavot, les grandes arabesques, les coussins et de la vapeur montante.

Le motif étranger le plus fréquent: le papayer.

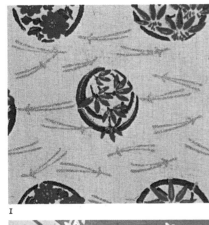

1

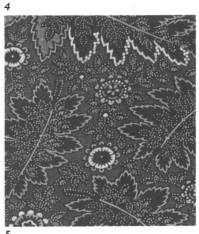

4

2

3

5

6

7

8

9

10

11

12

13

14

15

16

17

18

19

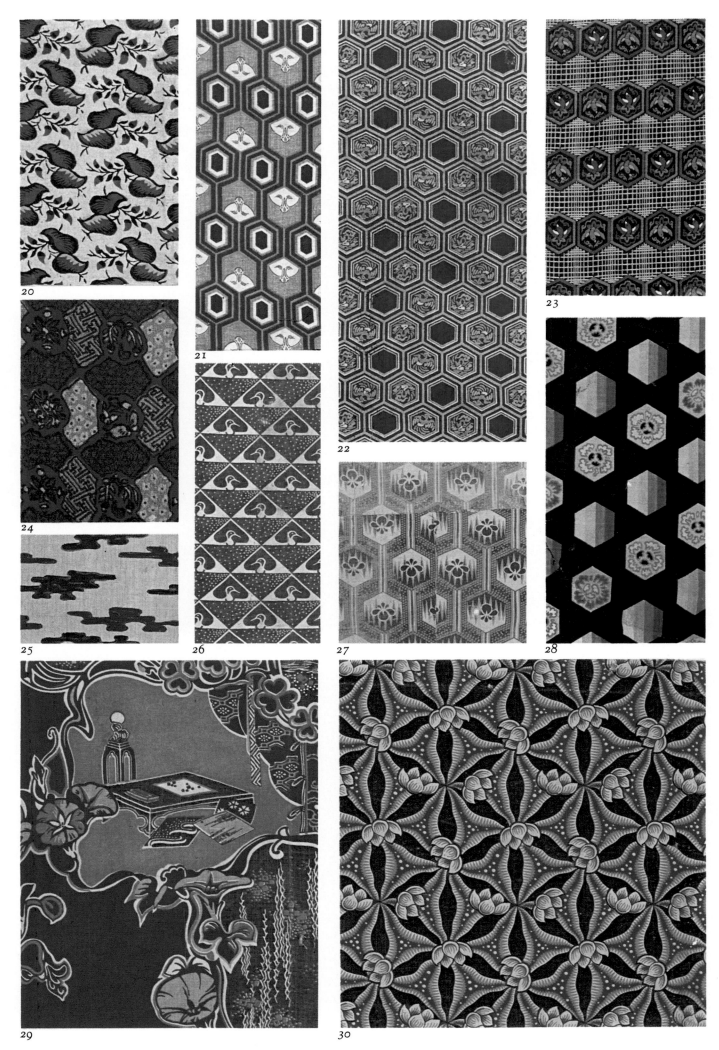

20

21

22

23

24

25

26

27

28

29

30

43

44

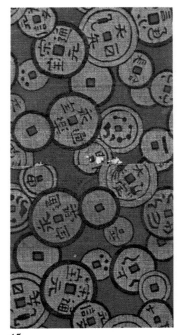

45

47

46

48

49

50

51

52

53

54

55

56

57

58

59

60

61

62

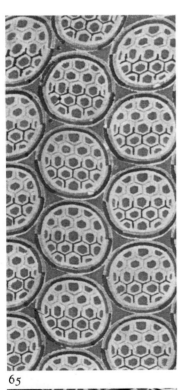

65

63

66

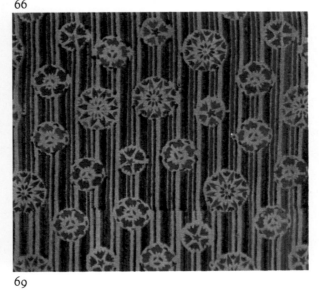

64

67

68

69

70

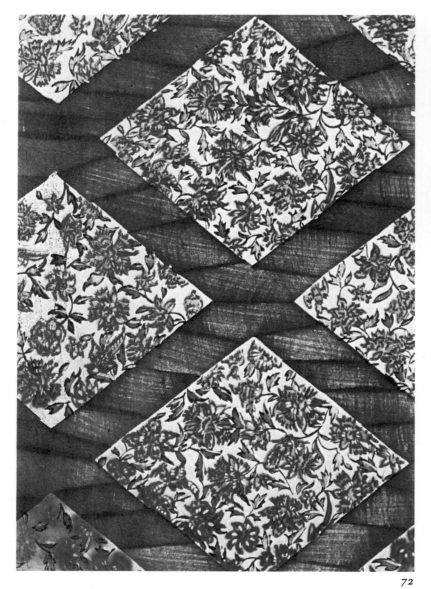

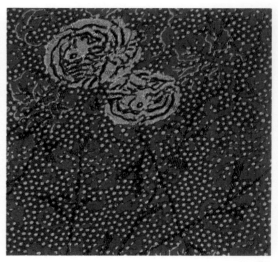

71

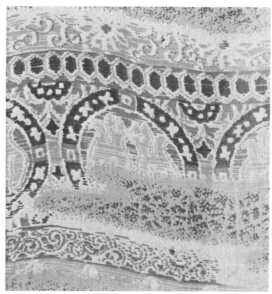

72

73

74

75

76

77

78

79

80

81

82

83

84

85

86

87

88

89

90

91

92

93

94

95

96

97

98

99

100

101

102

103

104

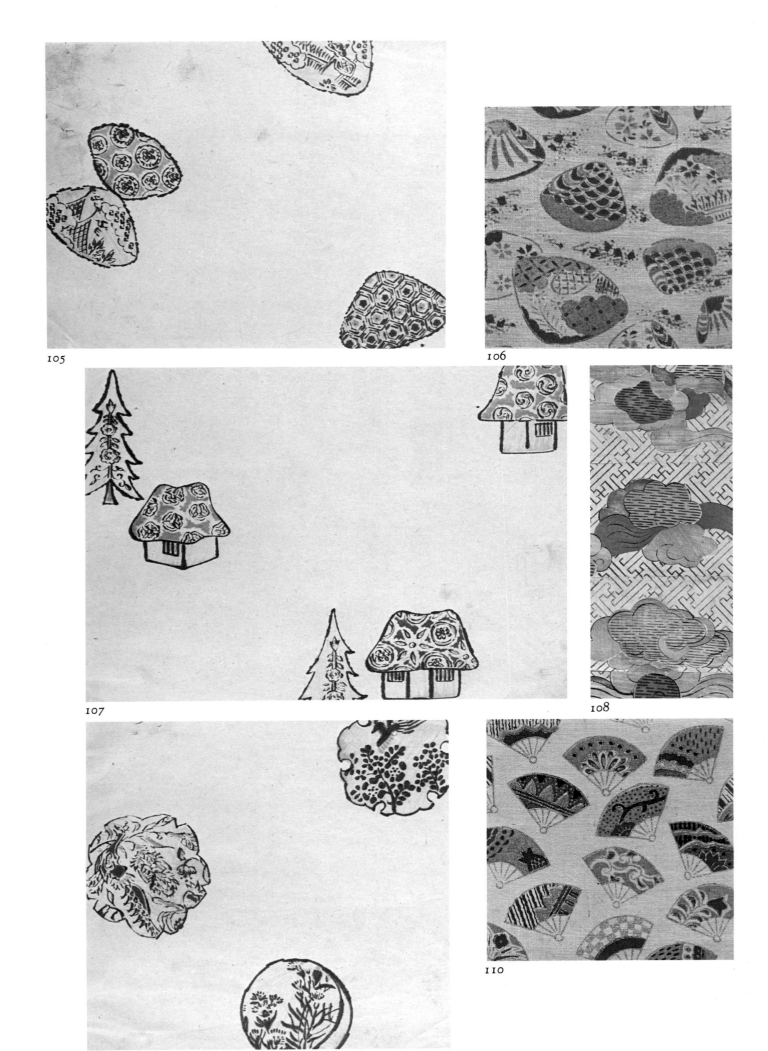

105

106

107

108

109

110

111

112

113 114

115

116 117 118

119

120

121

124

122

123

125

126

127

128

129

130

131

132

133

134

Patterns
with human figures and dolls

Muster
mit menschlichen Figuren und Puppen

Motifs
à figures humaines et poupées

Among these patterns we find series of a single motif as well as combinations of different variations on a motif. Talismans and depictions of religious scenes or legends are also especially popular. Beyond this there are often large patterns, considered unfit for clothing, which were very popular among the general population as wall hangings. Motifs included calendars, astrological signs, unearthly statues, cute dolls, pictures of foreigners, and caricatures of puppets.

The most often-used Japanese motifs are Chinese children, human chains, faces, dolls from Kyoto, toy dolls, and the seven Gods of Luck.

The foreign motifs most often encountered are mermaids, knights, Buddhas, Chinese children, small boys, and shadow pictures of dolls.

Unter diesen Mustern gibt es sowohl Serien eines einzigen Motives als auch Kombinationen verschiedener Motivvariationen. Besonders beliebt sind auch Talismane und Schilderungen von religiösen Szenen oder Erzählungen. Darüber hinaus gibt es häufig große Muster, welche zwar für Kleidungsstücke als unpassend empfunden wurden, als Wandbehang jedoch bei der einfachen Bevölkerung sehr beliebt waren. Als Motive wählte man Kalender, Sternzeichen, unheimliche Statuen, liebliche Puppen, Bilder von Ausländern oder Puppen-Karikaturen.

Häufigste Motive Japans: chinesische Kinder, Menschenketten, menschliche Gesichter, Puppen aus Kyoto, Spielzeugpuppen und die sieben Glücksgötter.

Die häufigsten ausländischen Motive: Meerjungfrauen, Reiter, Buddhas, chinesische Kinder, kleine Jungen, Schattenbilder von Puppen und Schauspielpuppen.

Il existe des séries d'un seul motif et des compositions réalisées à partir de variations des motifs. Les représentations de talismans et de scènes religieuses ou de récits étaient fréquentes ainsi que les grands motifs ne convenant pas aux vêtements mais très appréciés en tentures murales par les gens du peuple. Les motifs étaient choisis parmi les objets suivants: calendriers, signes du zodiaque, statues insolites, poupées mignonnes, images d'étrangers ou caricatures de poupées.

Les motifs japonais les plus fréquents sont: enfants chinois, chaîne humaine, visages humains, poupées de Kyoto, poupées en miniature et les sept dieux du bonheur.

Les motifs étrangers les plus fréquents: sirènes, cavaliers, bouddhas, enfants chinois, silhouettes de poupées et de poupées de kabuki.

6

7

8

9

10

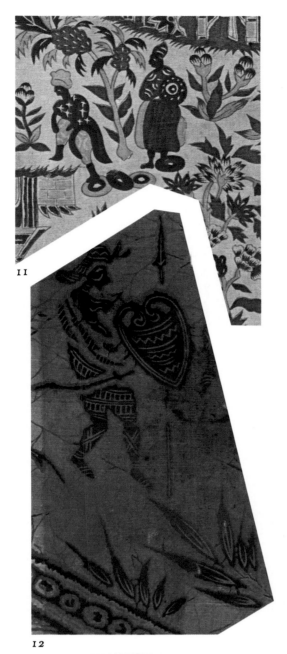

11

12

13

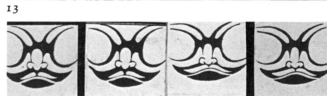

14

15

16

17

18

19

20

21

22

23

24

25

26

27

28

29

31

30

32

33

34

35

36

37

38

39

40

41

51

52

53

54

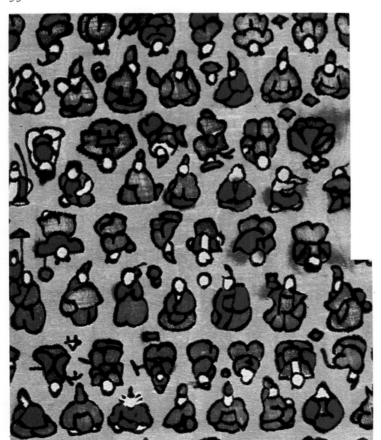

55

56

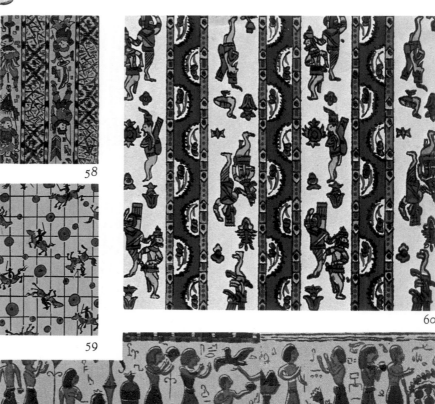

58

59

60

61

62

WATARI TE
copied patterns

WATARI-TE
kopierte Muster

WATARI-TE
motifs copiés

WATARI TE is the term for patterns which were originally brought to Japan by foreigners and then copied and adopted by the Japanese. The most common patterns soon merged with traditional Japanese designs (e.g. YUZEN) into WASARASA. But there are a few patterns which one can still clearly identify as original WATARI TE. WATARI TE, like arabesques and tile-like patterns from the Near and Middle East, have enjoyed great popularity in recent years.

The most often-used Japanese motifs are strawberries, raspberries, and patterns from Jakarta.

The foreign motifs most often encountered are arrays of boxes, grapevines, arabesques, mosaic patterns, tile-like arabesques, Bengalese and Persian motifs, melon trees.

Als WATARI-TE bezeichnet man Muster, die ursprünglich von Ausländern nach Japan gebracht und dann von den Japanern kopiert und übernommen wurden. Die gewöhnlichen Muster verflechteten sich bald mit den traditionellen japanischen (z.B. YUZEN) zu WASARASA. Dennoch existieren nach wie vor einige Muster, die unschwer als original WATARI-TE zu erkennen sind. In jüngster Zeit erfreuen sich gerade diese WATARI-TE-Muster sowie Arabesken und fliesenförmige Muster aus dem Nahen und Mittleren Osten wieder einer besonderen Beliebtheit.

Häufigste Motive Japans: Erdbeeren, Himbeeren und Jakarta-Muster.

Häufigste ausländische Motive: kassettenförmige Muster, Weinranken, Arabesken, Mosaik-Muster, fliesenförmige Arabesken, bengalische und persische Muster, Melonenbaum.

On appelle WATARI-TE les motifs qui ont été importés au Japon par des étrangers et qui furent ensuite copiés par les Japonais. Les motifs courants et les motifs japonais traditionnels (par ex. YUZEN) se fondirent bientôt en un motif WASARASA. Cependant il y a toujours quelques originaux de motifs WATARI-TE qui se reconnaissent facilement. Depuis peu ces motifs WATARI-TE connaissent un véritable regain d'intérêt au même titre que les arabesques, les motifs en forme de pavés originaires du Moyen- et Proche-Orient.

Motifs japonais les plus fréquents: fraises, framboises et motifs de Djakarta.

Motifs étrangers les plus fréquents: motifs en forme de cassettes, vrilles de vigne, arabesques, motifs en mosaïques, arabesques en forme de pavés, motifs bengalis et perses, papayers.

1

2

3

4

5

6

7

8

9

10

11

12

13

14

15

16

17

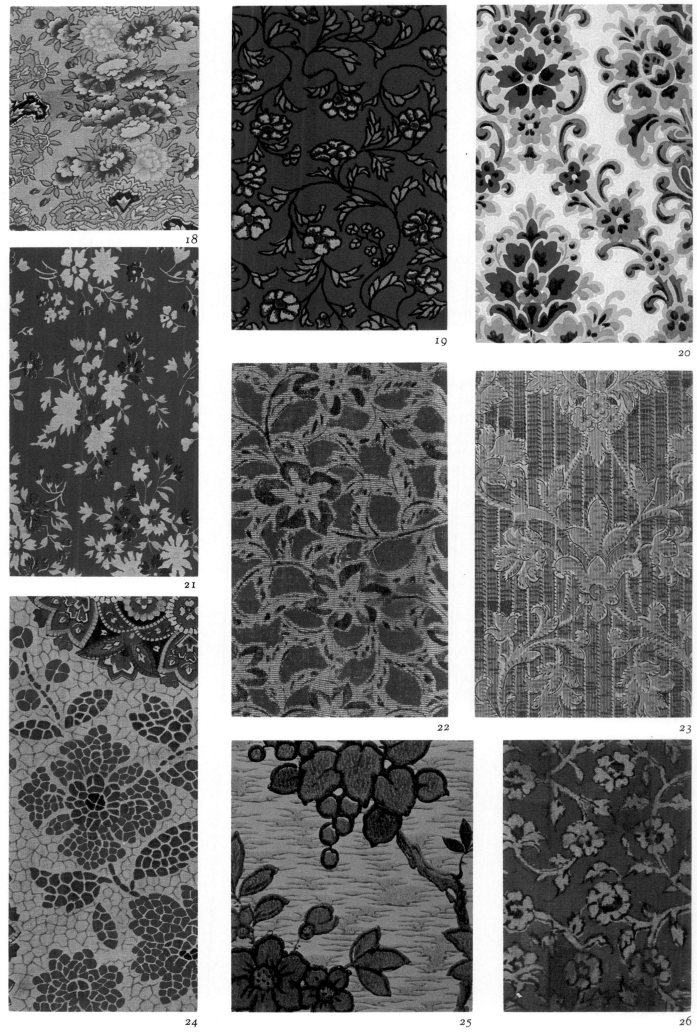

18

19

20

21

22

23

24

25

26

27

28

29

30

31

32

33

34

35

36

37

38

39

40

41

42

43

44

45

46

47

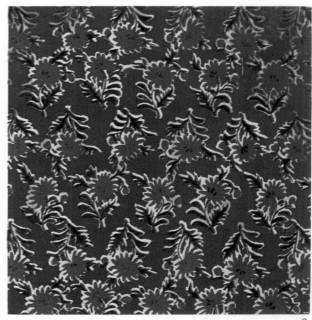

48

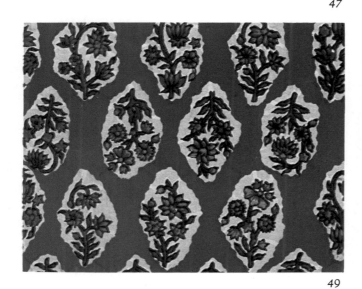

49

50

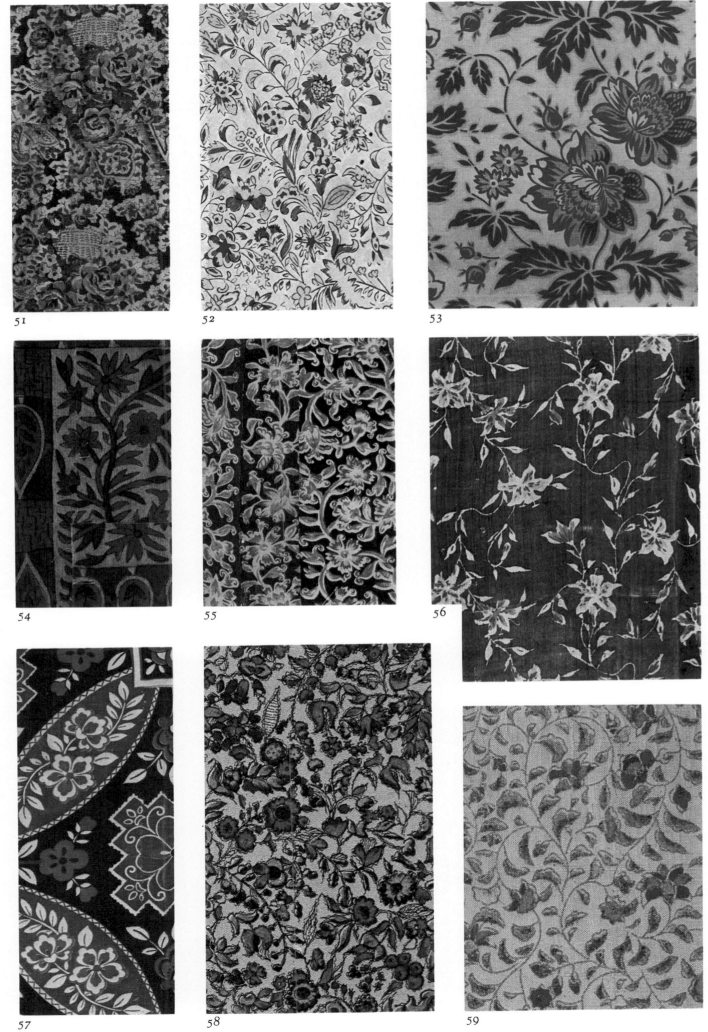

51

52

53

54

55

56

57

58

59

60

61

62

63

64

65

66

67

68

69

70

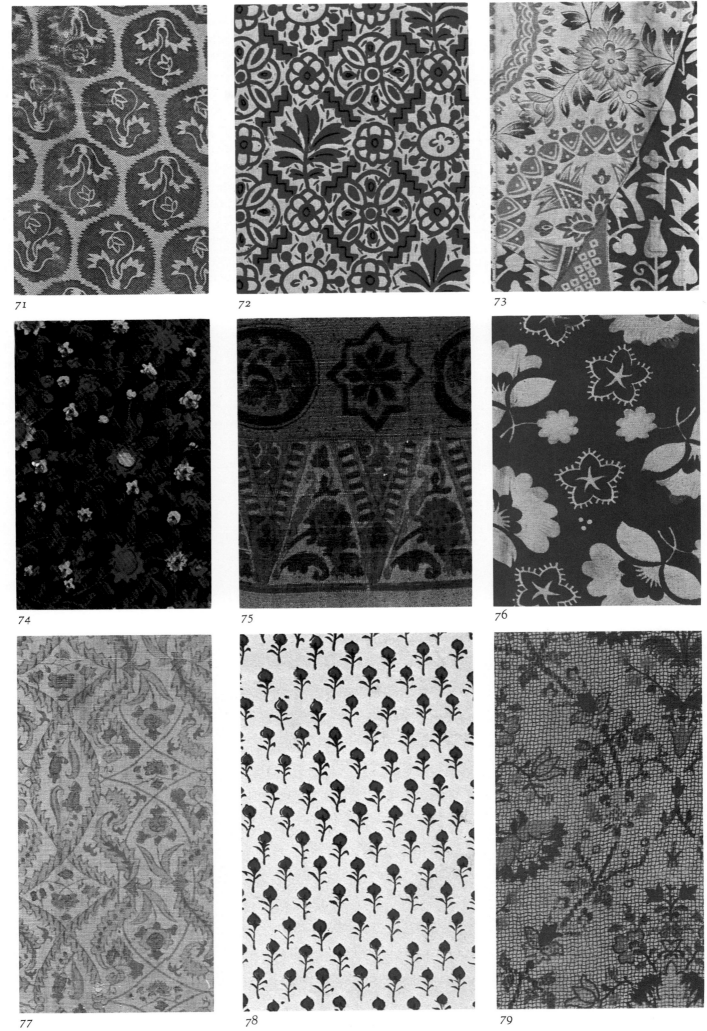

71

72

73

74

75

76

77

78

79

80

81

82

83

84

85

86

87

88

89

90

91

92

93

94

95

96

97

98

Patterns
with flowers and birds

Muster
mit Blumen und Vögeln

Motifs
à fleurs et à oiseaux

Birds and flowers are often used together in the same design, and sometimes also merge into a single mixed bird/flower organism. The sometimes wildly exaggerated birds and conspicuously stylised flowers convey the peculiar exoticism and fantastic atmosphere of WATARI textiles, and their romantic attraction is taken over as one of the main motifs of WATARASA.

The most often-used Japanese motifs are swallow, dove, sparrow, phoenix, magpie, eagle, pheasant.

The foreign motifs most often encountered are peacock, parakeet, firebird, wings.

Vögel und Blumen werden häufig gemeinsam für ein Muster verwendet und verschmelzen mitunter auch zu einer Mischform von Vogel und Blume. Die zum Teil übertrieben gezeichneten Vögel und auffälligen Blumen strahlen mit ihrer eigentümlichen Exotik die phantasievolle Atmosphäre der WATARI-Textilien aus und wurden mit ihrem romantischen Reiz als eines der Hauptmotive des späteren WASARASA übernommen.

Häufigste Motive Japans: Schwalbe, Taube, Sperling, Phönix, Elster, Adler und Fasan.

Häufigste ausländische Motive: Pfau, Sittich, Feuervogel und Flügel.

Les oiseaux et les fleurs sont souvent combinés et fusionnent en un composé de fleurs et d'oiseaux. Les oiseaux d'un dessin extrême et les fleurs spectaculaires reflètent avec leur exotisme singulier l'atmosphère pleine d'imagination des textiles WATARI et deviendront, par leur charme romantique, un des motifs principaux du futur WASARASA.

Motifs japonais les plus fréquents: hirondelle, pigeon, moineau, phénix, pie, aigle et faisan.

Motifs étrangers les plus fréquents: paon, perruche, oiseau de feu et ailes.

1

2

3

4

5

7

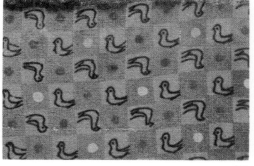

6

9

8

10

11

12

13

14

15

16

17

18

19

20

111

21

22

23

24

25

26

27

28

29

30

31

32

33

34

35

36

37

38

39

40

41

42

43

44

45

46

47

48

49

50

51

52

53

54

55

56

57

58

59

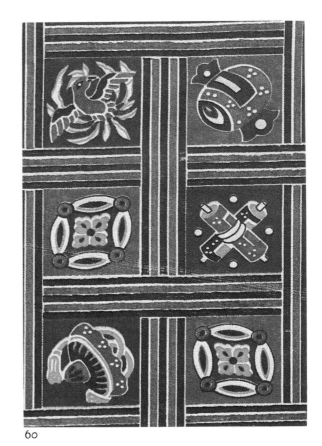

60

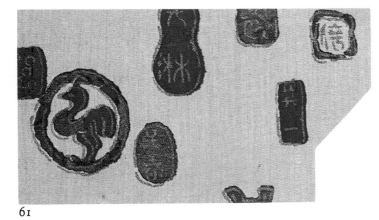

61

62

63

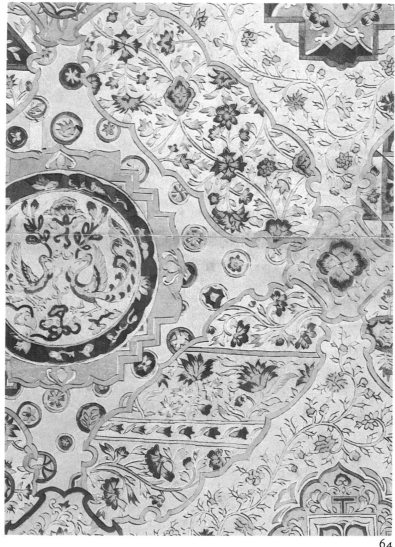

64

65

67

66

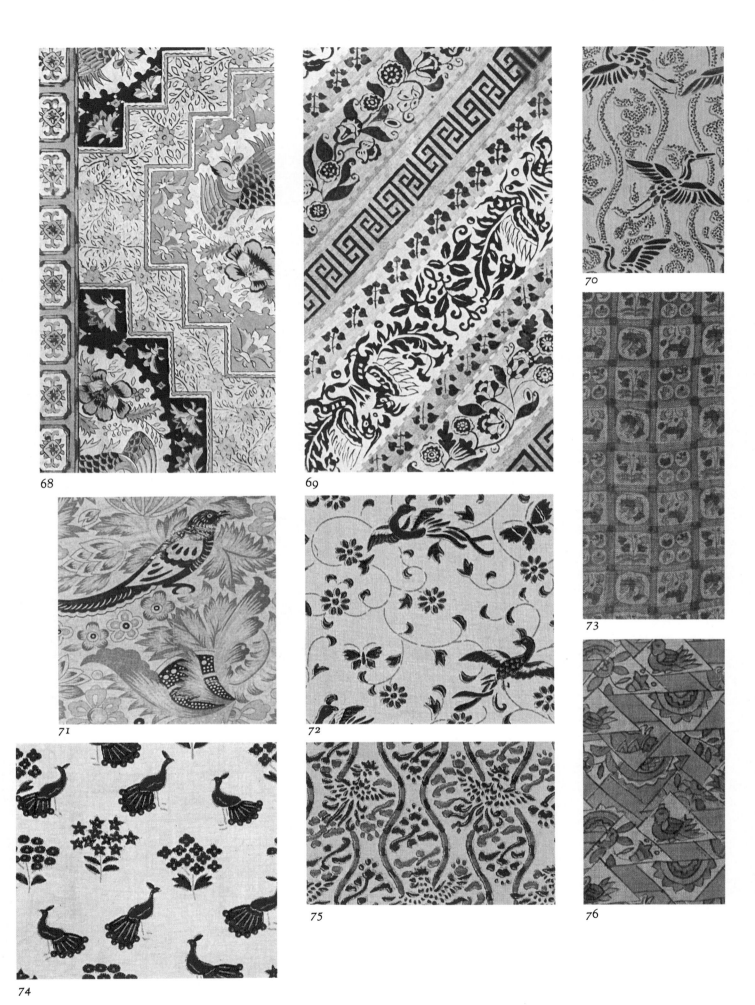

68

69

70

71

72

73

74

75

76

77

78

79

80

81

SAGARA TE
shaded patterns

SAGARA-TE
schattierte Muster

SAGARA-TE
motifs ombrés

SAGARA TE is not a kind of pattern, but a method by which known SARASA and other designs are shaded. This is accomplished through a series of tiny, closely-spaced circles that melt into the pattern and thus create an effect that sets off the actual motif and makes it appear more three-dimensional and lively. A similar technique is to be found in the art of Japanese embroidery and is called SAGARA. In that case, the same effect is achieved through tiny knots in the threads on the surface. The counterpart technique in metal engraving is called NANAKO. There, backgrounds and spaces not covered by the pattern are filled with tiny circles and points.

The most often-used Japanese motifs are poppies, points and circles, hail, snowflakes, sea anemones, small fragments, tiny seeds, graduated shades.

The foreign motifs most often encountered are SARASA with ferns, for example from Holland, France, and Russia.

SAGARA-TE selbst ist kein Muster, sondern eine Methode, mit welcher man bekannte Muster wie SARASA und dergleichen schattiert. Dies geschieht mit einer Serie von dicht gesetzten winzigen Kreisen, die mit den Mustern verschmelzen und somit die eigentlichen Motive herausheben und lebendiger erscheinen lassen. Vergleichbares findet man in der japanischen Stickkunst unter dem Namen SAGARA. Hier wird mit Hilfe von winzigen Garnknoten auf der Oberfläche des Stoffes die gleiche Wirkung erzielt. Ebenso wie in der Metallgravur, wo unter der Bezeichnung NANAKO die Hintergründe oder Zwischenräume der Muster mit kleinen Kreisen und Punkten gefüllt werden.

Häufigste Motive Japans: Mohn, Punkte und Kreise, Hagel, Schneeflocken, Seegurke, kleine Bruchstückchen, winzige Körner, abgestufte Schattierungen.

Häufigste ausländische Motive: SARASA mit Farnen, z.B. aus Holland, Frankreich, Russland.

Le SAGARA-TE n'est pas un motif mais une méthode consistant à ombrer les motifs connus comme le SARASA par exemple. Le dessin est recouvert de cercles minuscules qui fusionnent avec les motifs et font ainsi ressortir les vrais motifs tout en les animant. On trouve la même chose dans l'art de la broderie sous le nom de SAGARA. En ajoutant des nœuds de fils minuscules sur la surface, on obtient le même effet. De même qu'en gravure sur métal où le fond et les parties libres intermédiaires sont remplis avec des petits cercles et des points.

Motifs japonais les plus fréquents: pavot, points et cercles, grêle, flocons de neige, anémones de mer, petits morceaux, points minuscules, ombres nuancées.

Motifs étrangers les plus fréquents: SARASA avec des fougères de Hollande, de France et de Russie par exemple.

1

2

4

3

5

6

15

16

17

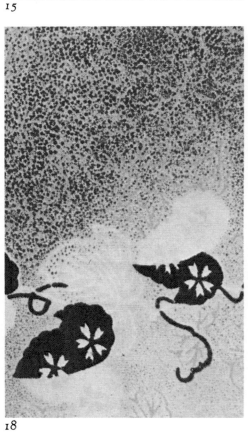

18

19

20

127

21

22

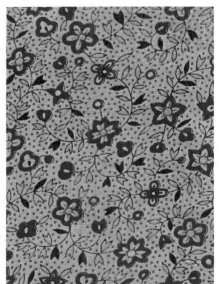

23

24

25

26

27

28

29

30

31

32

33

34

35

36

37

38

39

40

41

43

42

44

45

46

Patterns
with lines, stripes, diamonds and geometric shapes

Muster
mit Linien, Streifen, Karos und geometrischen Figuren

Motifs
à lignes, rayures, carreaux et figures géométriques

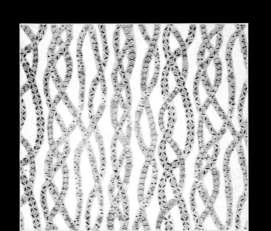

Designs using perpendicular lines, horizontal stripes, combinations of horizontal and perpendicular lines (lattice), diagonal stripes, parallel lines that twist around each other and the like, today count among traditional Japanese patterns. Nonetheless, they originally belonged to imported WATARI patterns and were named SHIMA. The written characters used for the word "SHIMA" nowadays are those which denote the phrase "striped pattern", but in earlier times the character for "island" (also pronounced SHIMA) was used to denote these patterns.

This book includes pictures only of SARASA striped patterns (sarasa shima) — diverse compositions of wild lines in typical SARASA colours, as well as geometric, symmetrical arabesques.

The most often-used Japanese motifs are stripes, emphatic lines, bars, loops, bamboo patterns, grids, cubes, stone walls, light effects, etc.

The foreign motifs most often encountered are bundled stripes, checkerboard, arabesques, triangles, S-chains, crosses, diamonds, etc.

Muster aus senkrechten Linien, horizontalen Streifen, Verflechtungen von waagerechten und senkrechten Linien (Gitter), diagonale Streifen, Verschlingungen nebeneinander verlaufender Linien und dergleichen zählen heute zu den traditionellen Mustern Japans. Ursprünglich gehörten sie jedoch zu den WATARI-Mustern und wurden als SHIMA bezeichnet. Während man heute SHIMA mit dem Schriftzeichen für „Streifenmuster" schreibt, benutzte man in früheren Zeiten das Zeichen für „Insel" (Aussprache ebenfalls SHIMA) zur Bezeichnung dieser Muster.

In diesem Buch finden sich ausschließlich Abbildungen von SARASA-Streifenmustern (sarasa-shima) — abwechslungsreiche Kompositionen wilder Linien in der typischen SARASA-Färbung sowie Arabesken aus geometrischen Mustern.

Häufigste Motive Japans: Streifen, unterstrichene Linien, Gitter, Schlingen, Bambus-Muster, Matten, Würfel, Steinmauern, Lichteffekte etc.

Häufigste ausländische Muster: Streifenbündel, Schachmuster, Arabesken, Triangel, „S"-Ketten, Kreuze, Karos etc.

Motifs composés de lignes verticales, horizontales, de lignes qui se croisent (grille), de rayures diagonales, d'entrelacements de lignes placées les unes à côté des autres; aujourd'hui ces figures font partie des motifs traditionnels du Japon. Ils appartenaient pourtant à l'origine aux motifs WATARI et étaient connus sous l'appellation SHIMA. Alors qu'aujourd'hui on écrit SHIMA avec les idéogrammes de «Motifs à rayures», on utilisait à l'époque pour désigner ces motifs les idéogrammmes de «île».

Dans ce livre on ne trouve que des reproductions de motifs à rayures SARASA (sarasa-shima), compositions de lignes débridées dans le coloris caractéristique SARASA ainsi que des arabesques de motifs géométriques.

Motifs japonais les plus fréquents: rayures, lignes soulignées, grille, boucle, bambons, nattes, dés, murs en pierre, effets lumineux etc...

Motifs étrangers les plus fréquents: faisceaux de lignes, motif à damier, arabesques, triangles, Chaînes de «S», croix, carreaux etc...

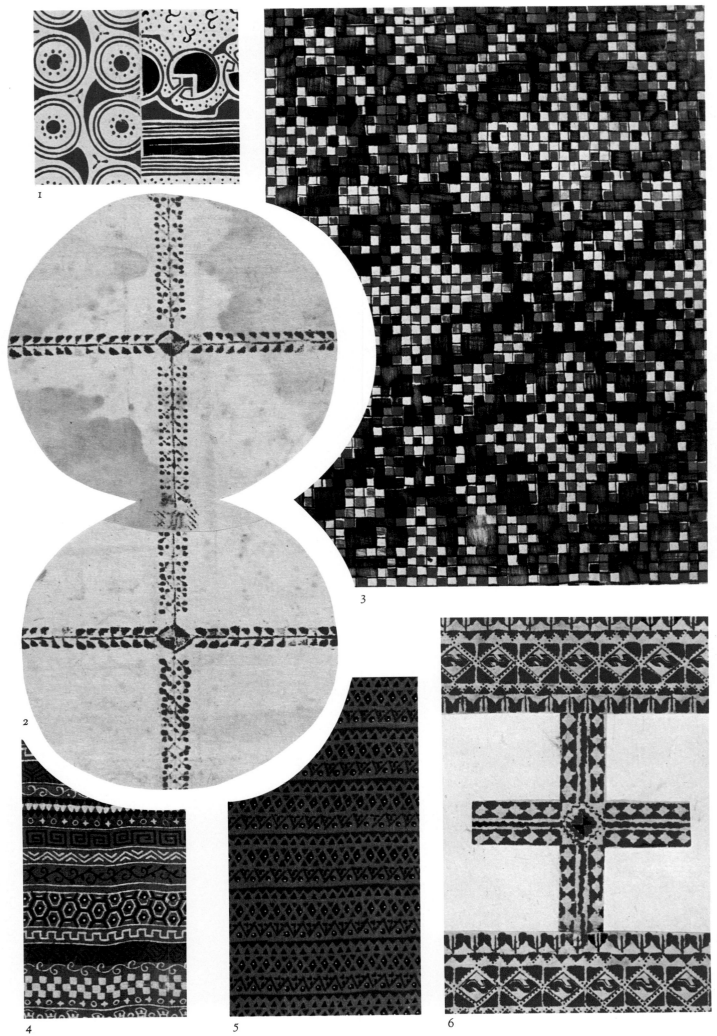

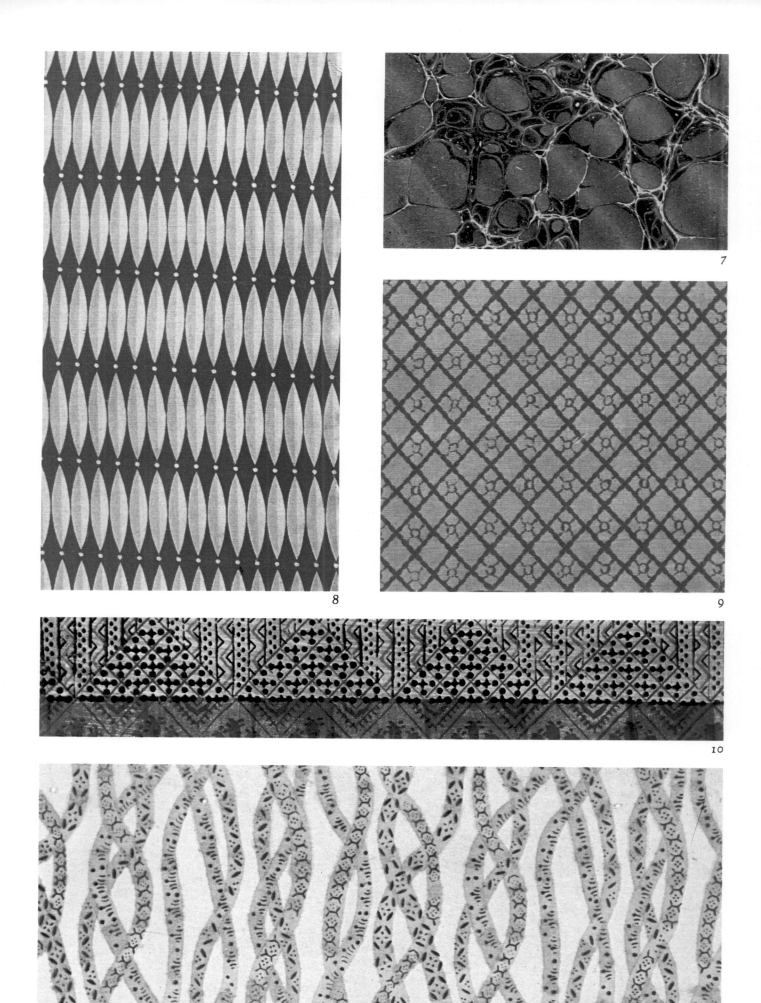

8

7

9

10

11

12

13

14

15

16

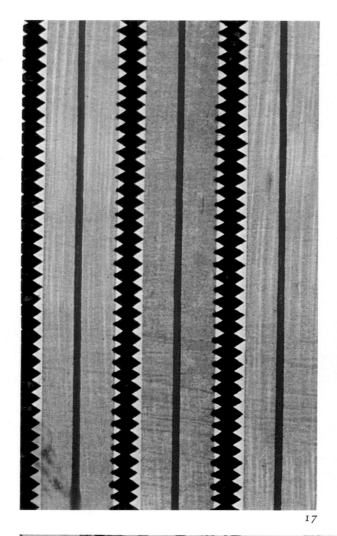

17

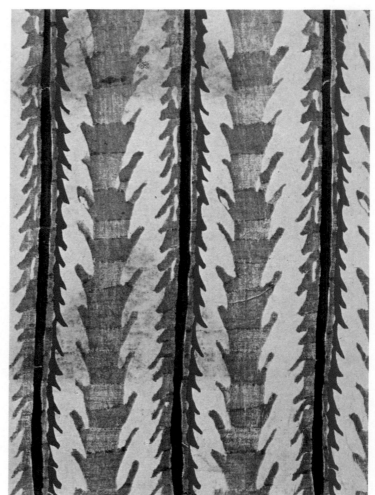

18

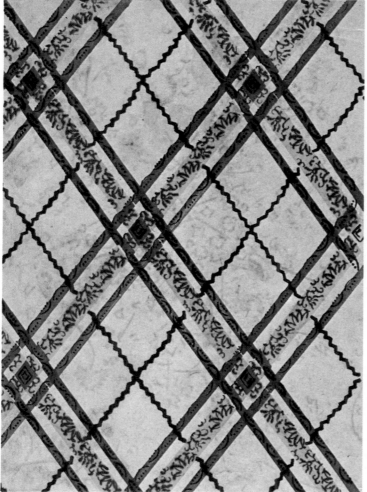

19

20

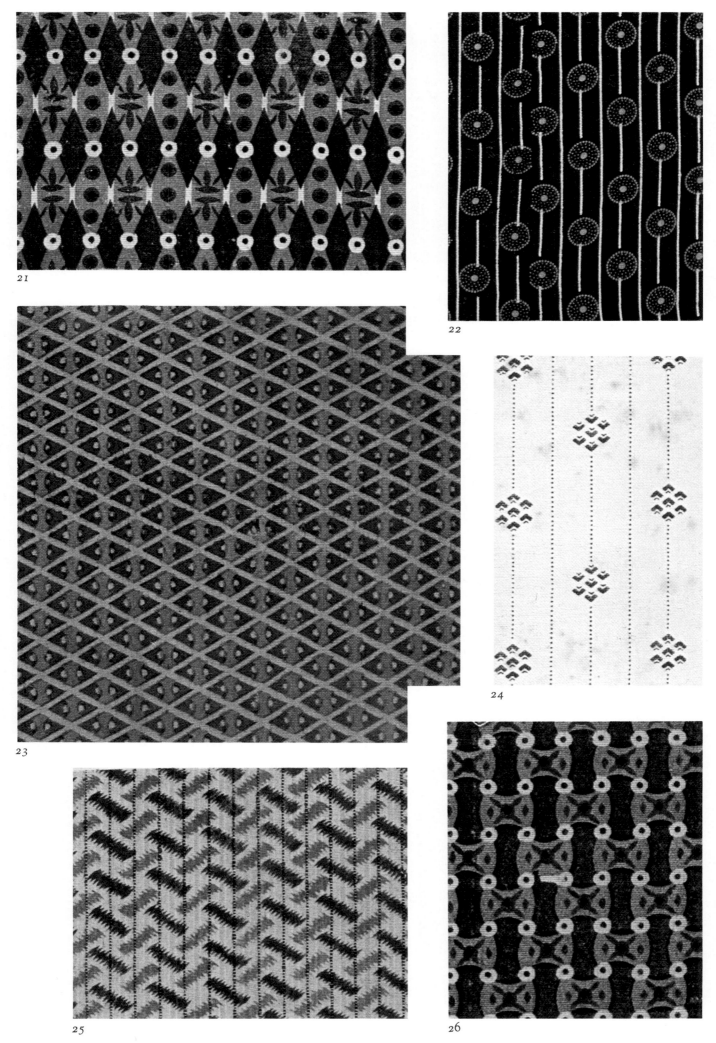

21

22

23

24

25

26

27

28

29

30

31

32

33

34

35

36

37

38

39

40

41

42

43

44

45

46

47

48

49

50

51

52

53

54

55

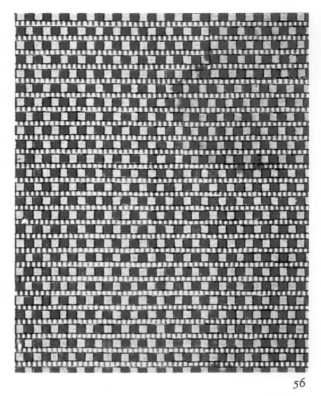

56

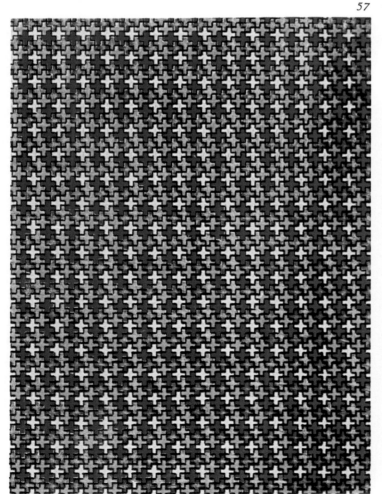

57

58

59

60

61

62

63

64

65

66

67

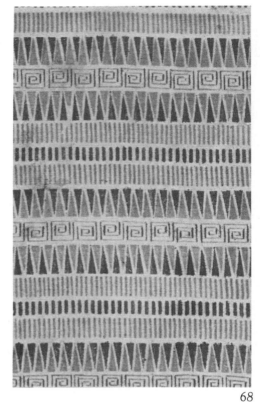

68

71

69

70

72

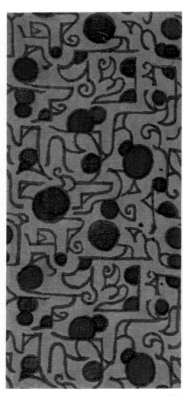

73

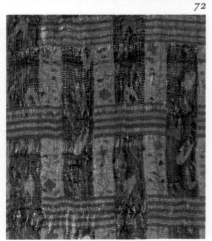

74

75

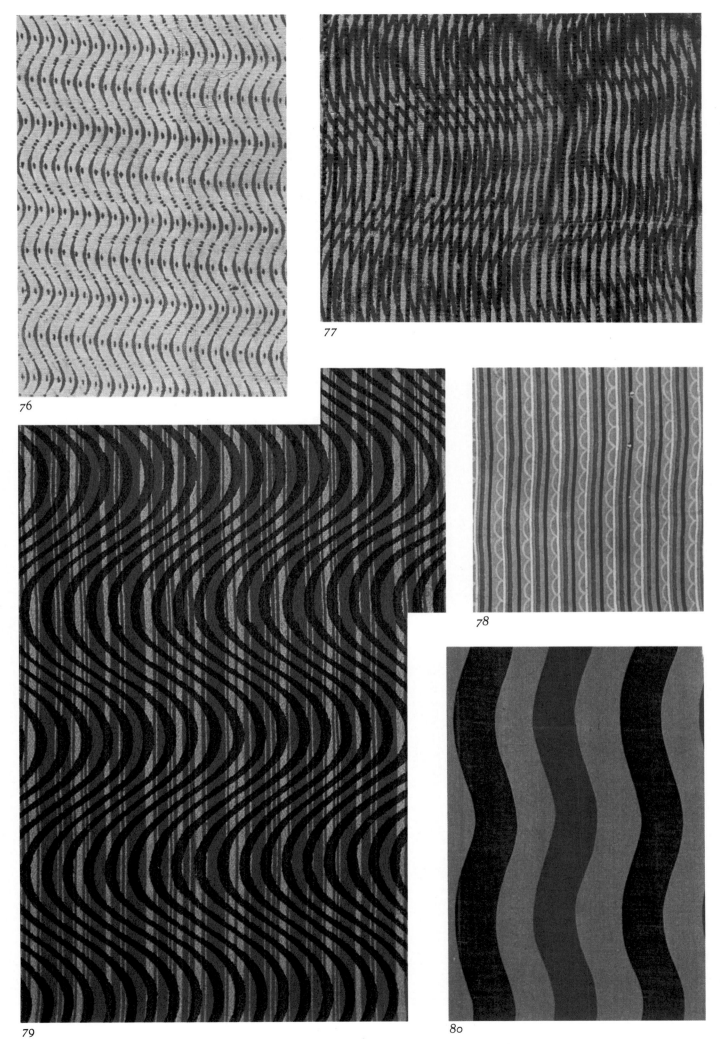

76

77

78

79

80

145

81

82

83

84

85

86

87

Patterns
with four-legged animals, insects and fish

Muster
mit vierbeinigen Tieren, Insekten und Fischen

Motifs
avec animaux quadrupèdes, insectes et poissons

In earlier times it was mostly four-legged animals and monsters that were to be found on the armour and JIMBAORI of field commanders. Butterflies, insects and fish were used for large patterns and decorated clothing, cloth belts, curtains, ceremonial costumes, and wall hangings. But today as well, one will often find attractive designs and original arrangements with various four-legged creatures, insects, or fish on Turkish and Persian rugs and, most recently, on traditional ladies' clothing, kimonos and occidental clothing worn by all population groups.

The most often-used Japanese motifs are rabbits, butterflies, Chinese animal symbols.

The foreign motifs most often encountered are lions, tigers, fire-spitting dragons, mythological animals, and reindeer, for example on cashmere shawls and oriental rugs.

In alten Zeiten schmückten meist vierbeinige Tiere oder Ungeheuer die Rüstungen und JIMBAORI der Feldherren. Schmetterlinge, Insekten oder Fische wurden für große Muster verwendet und dekorierten Kleidungsstücke, Stoffgürtel, Vorhänge, Festkleidungen oder Wandbehänge. Aber auch heutzutage findet man reizvolle Designs und originelle Arrangements mit verschiedenen Vierbeinern, Insekten oder Fischen auf türkischen und persischen Teppichen und – gerade in jüngster Zeit – auf traditioneller Damenbekleidung, Kimonos und abendländischen Kleidungsstücken aller Bevölkerungsschichten.

Häufigste Motive Japans: Kaninchen, Schmetterling, chinesische Tierkreiszeichen.

Häufigste ausländische Motive: Löwe, Tiger, feuerspeiender Drache, Fabeltiere und Rentier. Zum Beispiel auf Cashmere-Schultertüchern und Teppichen des Nahen und Mittleren Ostens.

Les armures et le JIMBAORI des généraux du passé étaient décorés de quadrupèdes. Papillons, insectes ou poissons étaient utilisés pour les grands motifs et ornaient les vêtements, les ceintures en tissu, les rideaux, le costume de fête ou la tenture murale. On trouve encore de nos jours de très beaux dessins et des arrangements originaux composés à partir d'animaux, d'insectes ou de poissons sur les tapis turcs et persans ainsi que depuis peu de temps sur les vêtements féminins traditionnels, les kimonos et les vêtements occidentaux de toutes les couches de la population.

Les motifs japonais les plus fréquents: lièvres, papillons, signes du zodiaque chinois.

Motifs étrangers les plus fréquents: lions, tigres, dragons crachant du feu, bestiaire fabuleux et rennes. Par exemple sur les châles de Cachemi et les tapis du Moyen- et Proche-Orient.

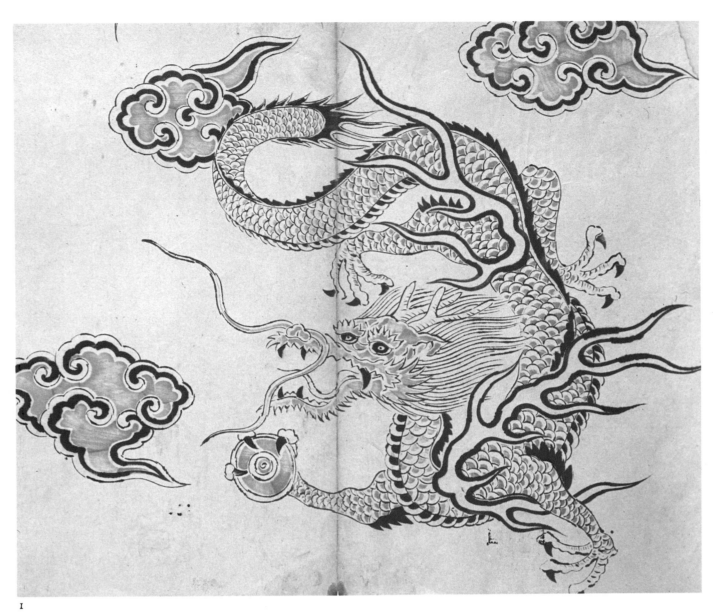

1

4

2

3

5

6

8

7

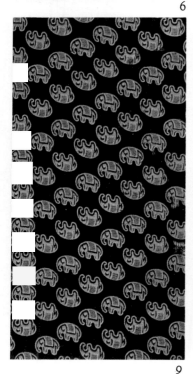

9

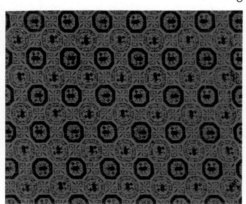

10

11

12

13

14

15

18

16

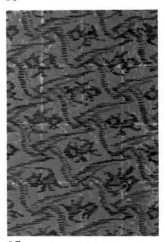

17

19

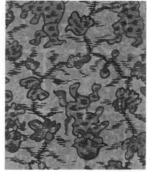

20

21

22

23

24

25

26

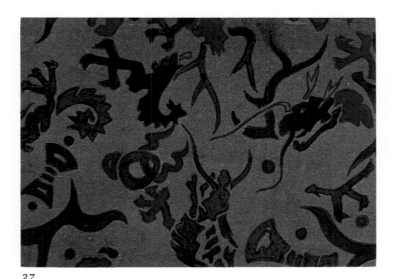

27

28

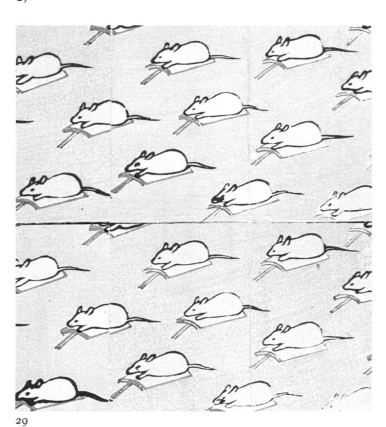

29

30

31

32

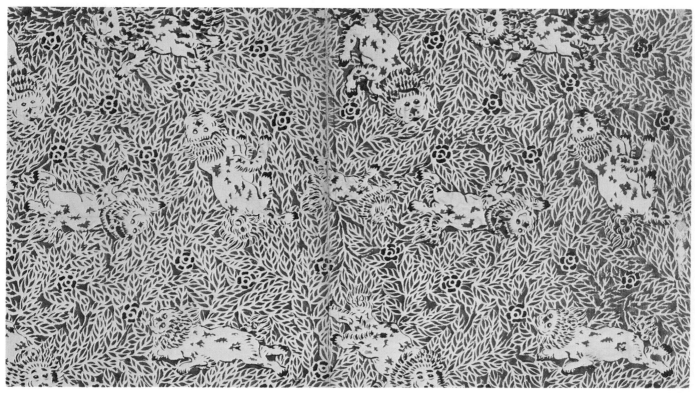

33

34

35

36

37

38

39

40

42

41

43

44

45

Notes on the numbering of the patterns

The illustrated patterns cre divided into nine groups. Every pattern within each group is numbered sequentially. This was done with the intent of allowing easy reference and comparison of the various patterns. The same numbers were employed as in the old pcttern book (MIHONCHO), also known as the TEITA numbers.

Hinweise zur Numerierung der Muster

Die abgebildeten Muster wurden in neun Gruppen eingeteilt. Innerhalb dieser Gruppen wurde jedem Muster eine fortlaufende Zahl zugeordnet. Dieses geschah mit der Absicht, ein Nachschlagen und Vergleichen unter den Mustern nach Möglichkeit zu erleichtern. Verwendet wurden dabei die gleichen Nummern, wie sie bereits in einem alten Musterbuch (MIHONCHO) erstellt wurden, die sogenannten TEITA-Nummern.

Quelques précisions sur la numérotation des motifs

Les illustrations de ce livre ont été classées en neuf groupes. Les motifs de chaque groupe ont été numérotés en continu pour permettre au lecteur de trouver plus facilement ceux des spécimens qu'ils désirent regarder. Pour cette raison nous avons choisi les numéros TEITA déjà utilisés dans un ancien album de motifs (MIHONCHO).

Appendix

The original edition of this book was first published in folio format on March 25th, 1976, under the title "WASARASA MOYO ZUKAN" (WASARASA Picture Book). As an authentic work on traditional WASARASA patterns, it soon found extensive use in the textile and porcelain industries. That means that this book was used as an inspiration and resource for the design of new patterns and materials. On the occasion of the fourth, expanded edition of November 1977, the folio form was abandoned and my long-standing wish for a less dear, popular edition was realised. With the intention of publishing an easy-to-handle book in a usual format, improvements of the illustrations were undertaken, a new sleeve was designed, and the format was simplified. This book in its current form, under the title "FUKYUBAN WASARASA MOYO ZUKAN", (Popular Edition of the WASARASA Design Picture Book), was the final result.

In conjunction with the publication of the popular edition, I wish to express my heartfelt gratitude to Mr. Toshiro Kuze of the firm Graphic-sha Co., Ltd., who did not hesitate to make great sacrifices to help bring the popular edition into being, and who has been very helpful to me from the very first edition.

Kamon Yoshimoto, May 1982

Nachwort

Die Erstausgabe dieses Buches erschien am 25.3.1976 mit dem Titel „WASARASA MOYO ZUKAN" (WASARASA-Bildband) im Folioformat. Als ein authentisches Werk über traditionelle WASARASA-Muster fand es weitreichende Verwendung in der Textil- und Porzellanindustrie. Man benutzte dieses Buch als Anregung und Quelle für die Gestaltung neuer Muster und Materialien. Anläßlich der vierten erweiterten Auflage im November 1977 wurde dieser Buchform jedoch ein Ende gesetzt und mein langgehegter Wunsch nach einer preiswerten Volksausgabe realisiert. In der Absicht, ein leicht zu handhabendes Buch im üblichen Format zu publizieren, wurden bei den Illustrationen Verbesserungen vorgenommen, ein neuer Umschlag gestaltet und das Format vereinfacht, so daß schließlich dieses Buch mit dem Titel „FUKYUBAN WASARASA MOYO ZUKAN" (Volksausgabe des Buches „WASARASA-Bildband") vorlag.

Anläßlich der Publikation dieser Volksausgabe möchte ich Herrn Toshiro Kuze von der Firma Graphic-sha Co.,Ltd. meinen tiefen Dank aussprechen, da er sich aufopfernd für diese Volksausgabe eingesetzt hat und mir seit der ersten Ausgabe bis heute sehr behilflich war.

Kamon Yoshimoto, Mai 1982

Postface

Ce livre a été publié pour la première fois le 25.3.1976 sous le titre «WASARASA MOYO ZUKAN» (WASARASA) en folio. Ouvrage sérieux et documenté sur les motifs WASARASA traditionnels, il a trouvé depuis sa parution de nombreuses applications dans l'industrie de la porcelaine et du textile où on s'en sert comme source d'inspiration pour créer de nouveaux motifs et matériaux. A l'occasion de la quatrième réédition du livre en 1977, ce livre a été publié dans une édition populaire, ce que je désirais depuis longtemps. Certaines améliorations durent être apportées dans l'illustration afin de rendre ce livre pratique à consulter, une nouvelle couverture fut conçue et le format simplifié. Le livre parut enfin sous le titre «FUKYUBAN WASARASA MOYO ZUKAN» (Edition populaire du livre «WASARASA»).

A l'occasion de la publication de cet ouvrage, je voudrais exprimer mes remerciements à Monsieur Toshiro Kuze de la Graphic-sha Co., Ltd., pour le concours qu'il a bien voulu m'accorder depuis la première parution de ce livre et sans qui celui-ci n'aurait pu être publié.

Kamon Yoshimoto, mai 1982

Short biography

Kamon Yoshimoto was born on April 5th, 1913. He researches ornaments and patterns and directs the Society for the Historical Research of Textiles.
His most important works include:

"Sample Collections of WASARASA Patterns of the Meiji Period", colour edition (print run limited to 60 copies), Kyoto Shoin Publications, February 1967.

"Popular Coloured Paper", colour edition (print run limited to 125 copies), Kyoto Shoin Publications, August 1967.

"SARASA Patterns on Paper", colour edition (print run limited to 12 copies), Kyoto Shoin Publications, January 1970.

"CHIYOGAMI Patterns", colour edition (print run limited to 120 copies), Kyoto Shoin Publications, April 1971.

"WASARASA Patterns on Textiles", colour edition (print run limited to 95 copies), Kyoto Shoin Publications, June 1971.

"EDOKOMON Sample Collection", colour edition (print run limited to 200 copies), December 1972

Kurzbiographie

Kamon Yoshimoto wurde am 5. April 1913 geboren. Er befaßt sich mit der Erforschung von Ornamenten und Mustern und leitet die Forschungsgesellschaft für alte Textilien.
Seine wichtigsten Werke sind:

„Mustersammlung der WASARASA-Muster aus der Meiji-Zeit", Farbausgabe (limitiert auf 60 Exemplare), Kyoto-Shoin-Verlag, Feb. 1967

„Volkstümliche Buntpapiere", Farbausgabe (limitiert auf 125 Exemplare), Kyoto-Shoin-Verlag, Aug. 1967

„SARASA-Muster auf Papier", Farbausgabe (limitiert auf 12 Exemplare), Kyoto-Shoin-Verlag, Jan. 1970

„CHIYOGAMI-Muster", Farbausgabe (limitiert auf 120 Exemplare), Kyoto-Shoin-Verlag, Apr. 1971

„WASARASA-Muster auf Textilien", Farbausgabe (limitiert auf 95 Exemplare), Kyoto-Shoin-Verlag, Juni 1971

„EDOKOMON-Mustersammlung", Farbausgabe (limitiert auf 200 Exemplare), Dez. 1972

Courte biographie de l'auteur

Kamon Yoshimoto est né le 5 avril 1913. Il est chercheur dans le domaine des ornements et des motifs décoratifs et dirige l'Association de la recherche sur les textiles anciens.
Principaux ouvrages:

«Collection de motifs WASARASA de l'ère Meiji», édition en couleurs (limitée à 60 exemplaires), Kyoto-Shoin, février 1967

«Papiers colorés populaires», édition en couleurs (limitée à 125 exemplaires), Kyoto-Shoin, août 1967

«Motifs SARASA», édition en couleurs (limitée à 12 exemplaires), Kyoto-Shoin, janvier 1970

«Motifs CHIYOGAMI», édition en couleurs (limitée à 120 exemplaires), Kyoto-Shoin, avril 1971

«Motifs WASARASA sur textiles», édition en couleurs (limitée à 95 exemplaires), Kyoto-Shoin, juin 1971

«Collection de motifs EDOKOMON», édition en couleurs (limitée à 200 exemplaires), décembre 1972